COUNTDOWN TO REFORM

COUNTDOWN TO REFORM

THE GREAT SOCIAL SECURITY DEBATE

REVISED AND UPDATED FOR 2001

HENRY J.
AARON

ROBERT D.
REISCHAUER

A CENTURY FOUNDATION BOOK
COSPONSORED BY THE BROOKINGS INSTITUTION

2001 • The Century Foundation Press • New York

The Century Foundation, formerly the Twentieth Century Fund, sponsors and supervises timely analyses of economic policy, foreign affairs, and domestic political issues. Not-for-profit and nonpartisan, it was founded in 1919 and endowed by Edward A. Filene.

LIBRARY OF CONGRESS CATALOGING-IN-PUBLICATION DATA

Aaron, Henry J.
  Countdown to reform : the great social security debate / by Henry J. Aaron and Robert D. Reischauer.—Rev. and updated for 2001.
     p. cm.
  Includes bibliographical references and index.
  ISBN 0-87078-462-5 (pbk. : alk. paper)
  1. Social security—United States—Finance.   I. Reischauer, Robert D. (Robert Danton), 1941–   . II. Title.
  HD7125 .A1774 2001
  368.4'301'0973—dc21

00-012725

Cover design by Claude Goodwin.
Manufactured in the United States of America.

FOREWORD

Compared to other rich nations, the United States does not provide very generous public programs for the elderly. The basic safety net, composed of Social Security and Medicare, for example, supplies lower benefit levels than those available in Western Europe. But these programs comprise the largest domestic activities undertaken by the U.S. government, touching more lives directly than anything else—save the income tax and the postal service.

Social Security especially has tended to operate with relatively little controversy, routinely accomplishing the task for which it was created—reducing poverty among the elderly. Without it, in fact, more than half of Americans over age 65 would fall below the poverty line. Now, however, with the retirement of America's largest generation—the baby boomers—in sight, both Social Security and health programs for the elderly are quickly moving to center stage in political and policy debates.

At one extreme, some are convinced—and they are trying hard to convince others—that more old people will be no blessing for the nation. They argue that America might be doomed to a sharply diminished future unless extreme steps are taken to change the way we provide for our aged. Others advise a more moderate course, adjusting burdens and benefits within the framework of the existing system. Not surprisingly, the differences in approach often reflect a more fundamental divergence on general questions about the proper role of government and about the interaction between market capitalism and the lives of individual citizens.

These competing ideas about how to make the necessary adjustments in retirement programs thus have become staples in broader public policy conversations in Washington and across the nation. The outcome is far from settled.

Overall, however, it seems clear that while societies everywhere are converging in a belief that high rates of economic growth and long-term prosperity are possible only with free markets, they also are learning (or, in the case of the United States, relearning) lessons about the risks that accompany free enterprise. These lessons underscore the continuing importance of building strong, democratic governmental institutions to enforce the rules of the game and to deal with the abuses of the marketplace. Moreover, the unavoidable uncertainty about the long-term outcome for any individual of a lifetime of work, savings, and investment confirms the indispensability of a reliable social safety net, especially for the young and old.

With so much at stake for so many, The Century Foundation has been supporting and publishing a wide array of analyses of the aging of America. On Social Security alone, we have published both Robert M. Ball's *Straight Talk about Social Security* and *Insuring the Essentials: Bob Ball on Social Security;* Robert Eisner's *Social Security: More, Not Less;* and multiple editions of our extremely popular Basics pamphlet, *Social Security Reform,* as well as *Beyond the Basics: Social Security Reform,* a volume of essays edited by Richard C. Leone and Greg Anrig. We also have set up a website providing information on this critical issue: www.socsec.org. We have been joined in our efforts by other organizations and individuals whose work has added to our understanding of the issues involved in retirement security.

In these efforts, a few experts stand out as exceptional for the breadth and depth of their knowledge and the fairness of their approach. Henry J. Aaron of The Brookings Institution and Robert D. Reischauer of The Urban Institute are in this elite class. The opportunity to make possible the publication in 1998 of their analysis and conclusions about how to save Social Security was one of the high points of our efforts to bring more light to this important debate. That edition of *Countdown to Reform* was published in the midst of heated arguments about the future of the program. The heady pace of the stock market then seemed to offer a sure way for all citizens to be rich—if the government would just get out of the way. The misunderstanding embedded in this sort of argument for privatizing Social Security was profound, as the volatility in the market as 2000 drew to a close has made all too clear. (Just how devastating would the effects of retiring during such a downturn be, especially to someone who had put a great deal of faith in technology stocks?) What was needed then to put the discussion back on track was an authoritative and comprehensive examination of the program and its strengths and weaknesses, as well as an assessment of the various reform proposals under discussion. Henry Aaron and Robert Reischauer fulfilled all those needs and more.

Now, in 2001, we are undoubtedly on the verge of a new and possibly even more important national debate about what to do about Social Security. It is a good bet that we soon shall be surrounded by a swirl of half-truths and outright howlers about how to "fix" the nation's premier social program. And here again, like an intellectual cavalry, are Aaron and Reischauer riding to the rescue with a new edition of their definitive work on the subject.

In the pages that follow, Aaron and Reischauer clearly lay out the basics about the impact of the boomers on the Social Security system. They sort through the major proposals that have been made to deal with the challenge of more elderly. And in an objective but blunt fashion, they assess the strengths and weaknesses of each alternative. Finally, they make a compelling case for their own synthesis of the best elements of a reform program. In one volume, in other words, there is just about everything an informed citizen needs to know about what is right and what is wrong with Social Security and how to preserve the system for the future.

In the end, of course, the authors stress that there is no magic formula that will sweep away all the issues raised by the aging of the boomers. For all but a few fortunate individuals, as well as for the nation as a whole, many questions (like life's risks in general) cannot be wished or legislated away. Given the long-term nature of the implicit contract involved in a retirement program (perhaps sixty years from the start of work to the end of life), such risks are inevitable. Over such a span, birthrates and medical progress are unpredictable, securities markets are sure to experience immense volatility, and even the most stable democracies are likely to experience sweeping transformations in politics and policy. In other words, the future development of society will remain complex and uncertain. When combined with the uncertainties intrinsic to the careers and health of individual workers, the case that the authors make for a safe and conservative social insurance program seems eminently sensible.

Social Security is far from perfect, but as the old joke reminds us, it—like old age itself—has a considerable edge over the alternatives. On behalf of the Trustees of The Century Foundation, I thank Henry Aaron and Robert Reischauer for their exceptional contribution to our thinking about how to save Social Security.

RICHARD C. LEONE, *President*
The Century Foundation
January 2001

CONTENTS

LIST OF BOXES

List of Tables

LIST OF FIGURES

AUTHORS' PREFACE
TO THE SECOND EDITION

Since the first edition of this book appeared in December 1998, reform of Social Security has moved center stage in U.S. political debate. The major party candidates presented sharply different visions of Social Security during the 2000 presidential campaign. George W. Bush pledged repeatedly to push the introduction of individual accounts as a partial replacement for traditional Social Security. During the campaign, he said that he would earmark a portion of current payroll taxes to fund these accounts. This approach has elicited support from many Republicans and some Democrats. Vice President Gore called instead for buttressing the current system. Polls indicated that more Americans favored his position than supported Bush's. Proponents of this view point out that diverting payroll taxes from Social Security deepens the deficit in traditional assured benefits. They fear that diverting revenues will necessitate massive benefit cuts that are unlikely to be fully offset by accumulations in individual accounts.

The size of the stakes of the upcoming debate on Social Security reform can hardly be exaggerated. Its outcome will determine the form of the nation's basic pension plan for decades to come, with far-reaching economic and political implications.

Against this background, we felt it important to revise and update the first edition of *Countdown to Reform: The Great Social Security Debate*. As in the first edition, we describe major reform proposals and assign grades to them. The roster of reform plans in this second edition is almost entirely new. Some plans pass with honors, but others receive low marks or grades of incomplete—including the proposals of both major party presidential candidates. We examine the desirability of using general revenues to support Social Security or to underwrite the transition to individual accounts. We paid no attention in the first edition to this option because, as recently as just two years ago, we still found the prospect of large budget surpluses, except in Social Security, hard to take seriously. Now, a long run of budget surpluses seems likely, provided that Congress can resist passing large tax reductions and spending increases. The existence of such surpluses opens up possibilities for reform of the current Social Security system or for covering the costs of transition to a system of private accounts that did not exist when we wrote the first edition.

As in the first edition, we emphasize the importance of preserving the current defined-benefit system as the only way to assure basic income to retirees, survivors, and the disabled. We emphasize the importance of boosting national saving. We suggest that it is desirable and possible to boost the returns that workers receive on their payroll taxes. We show how to achieve that objective without incurring undesirable risks and needless administrative costs that are inescapable with individual account plans. But our main purpose is to provide information that will enable readers to judge for themselves what reforms in Social Security will best serve the interests of the nation over the coming decades.

We wish to acknowledge the financial support of The Century Foundation. We are grateful to our research assistants for help in updating and correcting the second edition. Along with all others who try to do research on the Social Security system, we are massively indebted to Stephen Goss, who was Deputy Chief Actuary during the period when we were revising the manuscript. His cost estimates are the "gold standard" on which all analysts depend, and his strict and scrupulously fair analytical observations should be ignored by no one.

ACKNOWLEDGMENTS

The authors wish to thank Robert Ball, Barry Bosworth, Gary Burtless, Peter Diamond, William Gale, Edward M. Gramlich, and Jack Triplett for reviewing drafts of the manuscript and making helpful suggestions. Jason Altman, Felicitie Bell, Bob Bonnette, Claudia Goldin, Kenneth Keppel, Helen Lazenby, Olivia Mitchell, Steve Ruggles, and Joshua Weiner provided guidance on data sources. Stephen Goss of the Social Security Administration provided the actuarial estimates that appear in Chapter 6. Stacie Carney, Jennifer Eichberger, Amanda Packel, Shanna Rose, and Jim Sly provided research assistance and fact checking. Kathleen Elliott Yinug provided secretarial support.

1

INTRODUCTION

The oldest of the baby boomers—those born between 1946 and 1964—will become eligible for Social Security retirement benefits during George W. Bush's last year in office, if he serves two terms. Three years later they will qualify for Medicare. When all the boomers have retired, roughly three decades later, more than 70 million former workers and their dependent spouses will have become Social Security beneficiaries.

Most Americans understand that Social Security's immediate situation is far from parlous. The program's income—from payroll and other tax revenues and the interest earned on the reserves accumulated in the trust fund—exceeded outlays for benefit payments and administration by a whopping $150 billion in 2000. Before the first of the baby boomers draws a benefit check, surpluses like these should boost Social Security's trust fund reserves from $1 trillion in 2000 to well over $2 trillion.

Is this merely the calm before the baby boomer storm? Clearly, no. Program income is currently expected to exceed spending until 2024. Such income supplemented by resources drawn from the trust fund's accumulated reserves should be sufficient to pay all currently promised benefits until 2037 or beyond.

But the lack of an immediate or even an intermediate-term crisis does not mean that all is well. The program faces significant longer-term

1

deficits. These shortfalls result not just from the retirement of baby boomers, but also from the anticipated increase in life expectancies and the reduced fertility rates that will lower the growth of the future workforce that will be paying the payroll taxes that support the program. If nothing at all were done to modify the current system until the trust funds were exhausted, and if current economic and demographic projections were to prove accurate, benefits would have to be cut by about one-fourth or payroll taxes would have to be increased by about 38 percent starting in the late 2030s. By 2075 the benefit cuts would have to grow to nearly one-third or the tax increase to 50 percent to keep the program afloat.

Social Security's financial balance could be maintained for the next seventy-five years, the period used for long-run Social Security planning, by immediately implementing less drastic adjustments—trimming benefits by about 12 percent or boosting payroll taxes 15 percent. Such action *could* resolve Social Security's long-run financial problem without requiring fundamental change to the program's structure.

The dominant characteristics of financial projections, however, are their uncertainty and volatility. From 1990 to 1997 the projected long-term deficit in Social Security more than doubled. Since 1997, the booming U.S. economy has reduced it by 15 percent, and the continuing strength of the economy promises further reductions. The long-run projections are acutely sensitive to small changes in developments that are impossible to forecast reliably—how fast worker productivity will increase, how fast mortality rates will decline, what will happen to interest rates, how many children people will have, and how many immigrants will enter the United States. Were economic performance to sour, the long-term deficit could turn out to be considerably larger than current projections indicate. With continued strong economic performance and favorable trends in other variables, it could turn out to be much smaller or could even disappear.

For this reason, the United States faces a larger and much more important question than how to deal with a projected financial shortfall nearly four decades into the future. It is whether the structure of Social Security, a program that is now 65 years old and was designed for a nation radically different from contemporary America, *should* be fundamentally changed. A debate on whether a program designed during the Great Depression is still the right program for twenty-first century America would be worthwhile even if Social Security's long-term finances were entirely adequate. When Congress passed the

Social Security Act in 1935, the most pressing problems were double-digit unemployment and pervasive poverty. Most families were struggling just to put food on the table and pay the rent; retirement saving was an unaffordable luxury for all but a privileged few. Almost three-quarters of workers had not graduated from high school. Fewer than one-fourth of women worked outside the home. Fewer than one in six marriages ended in divorce. More than one-fourth of 55- to 64-year-old women were widowed, and only 51 of every 100 men who reached 50 years of age lived to celebrate their 75th birthdays. Few retirees other than those who had worked for the railroads received a pension. Private financial institutions were shaky and financial markets were unstable and underdeveloped. Mutual funds did not exist. Individual Retirement Accounts, 401(k) plans, and Keogh plans—the instruments of "tax-sheltered" retirement saving—had not been invented because few families—fewer than 6 percent—paid income taxes from which they might wish to be sheltered.

The contemporary economy is stronger and far more stable. Most families have discretionary income—that is, resources beyond those needed for food, clothing, and shelter—some of which can be devoted to retirement saving. Some 56 percent of the workforce has at least some education past high school. Almost three-fifths of women age 16 and over are in the paid labor force, and two-earner couples are the norm. Seven of ten families pay personal income taxes. About half of marriages end in divorce, and fewer than one in seven (13 percent) of women between the ages of 55 and 64 are widowed. A bit more than half of all private sector workers are covered by an employer- or union-sponsored pension plan. Financial markets remain volatile but are strong and responsive to investors' wants. Slightly less than half of the population has experience with some sort of tax-sheltered saving account.

The two issues—how to deal with a projected long-term deficit and whether to change the structure of the existing system—are, of course, interrelated. There is little doubt that a perception of financial crisis heightens the willingness of the electorate to consider sweeping change. As often occurs during presidential campaigns, competing proposals sharpen, even if they do not always clarify, such complex issues. The 2000 presidential contest was no exception. During the campaign, George W. Bush called for the establishment of individual retirement accounts financed by payroll taxes diverted from Social Security. He claimed that the pensions financed by these personal accounts would fully offset the benefit cuts that would be needed to balance the Social Security system. Al Gore advocated retention of the current structure of Social Security and the use of a portion of surpluses projected for the non-Social Security budget to bolster the Social Security trust fund. Although he released few details during the campaign, Bush's proposal appears to require large benefit cuts for most active workers. The Gore proposal, on the other hand, would close only a bit more than half of the projected long-term deficit.

WHY YOU SHOULD READ THIS BOOK

With the 2000 election campaign over, the debate about how to reform Social Security can move forward to legislative proposals, congressional hearings, interest group position papers, and votes. The stakes in the outcome are enormous. Practically everyone pays Social Security taxes, receives benefits, or lives with someone who does. Some 154 million Americans paid $491 billion in Social Security taxes in 2000. Some 45 million Americans received retirement, disability, or survivor benefits.

Policymakers will have to decide when and how to address Social Security's projected long-term deficit and whether a new system could better meet the retirement income needs of the nation's elderly. Should Congress replace a program that has been on the books for more than six decades with one of the many proposed alternatives? Or should it close the projected long-term deficit while preserving Social Security's basic structure? The upshot of this debate will affect the economic security of most Americans for decades.

Almost everyone acknowledges that Social Security has been an enormous success in providing the elderly, the disabled, and survivors with a modest basic income. While benefits are far from generous—an average earner retiring at age 62 receives a benefit only slightly above the official poverty threshold—nearly two-thirds of elderly beneficiaries receive more than half of their total incomes from Social Security. Without Social Security, the incomes of approximately 12 million people—about 37 percent of all people 65 or older—would fall below official poverty thresholds. While the program is complex and deals with more than 6 million employers, 45 million beneficiaries, and more than 150 million taxpayers, its administrative costs are very low—less than 1 percent of retirement and survivor pension payments—well below those of private pension and insurance plans.

But the achievements of the past are no guarantee of future accomplishments. Moreover, the enormous changes in the nation since Social Security was enacted mean that the strengths of the current system should not preclude searching for something even better. And Social Security's projected long-term deficit means that some change is unavoidable. We should keep the current system if, but only if, we believe, first, that the United States still needs a mandatory savings plan to assure that individuals have basic incomes when they retire, become disabled, or lose a breadwinner to premature death; and, second, that continuation of Social Security is better than switching to any alternative.

Unfortunately, good information to help an interested citizen make sense of the debate on Social Security reform is hard to come by. The current program, although familiar, is very complicated and not well understood by most people. (To underscore this reality, we have provided a few basic questions about the current system in Box 1–1, page 6. The answers may surprise you.) The sound-bite portions of information served up by newspapers, magazines, and television are often incomplete and sometimes misleading or inaccurate. The rhetoric of the campaign sharpened some issues but was designed to persuade, not necessarily to inform. Unfortunately, expert participants in the debate are often unintelligible when they discuss reform proposals.

We have written this book to help you better understand the issues involved in the debate and to allow you to participate more constructively in the discussion. An important objective of the chapters that follow is to help you tune up your "BS meter," the instrument all sensibly skeptical observers should keep handy when listening to debates on complex and politically charged issues. As the debate unfolds, you, as interested members of the public, must continually ask yourselves, "Are the supposed 'facts' presented by the various advocates accurate?" "Are claims for the wonderful or catastrophic consequences of some new or old policy plausible?" and "Which of the sometimes conflicting values that different proposals promote matter most to me?"

Both of us have been involved with Social Security policymaking for many years and, not surprisingly, have developed some fairly strong

---

BOX 1–1
SOME BASIC FACTS ABOUT SOCIAL SECURITY

The vast majority of Americans have only a general familiarity with Social Security. They know that payroll taxes are deducted from their paychecks to support the program and that they can receive benefits after they reach age 62 that are adjusted each year to compensate for inflation. Beyond these facts, the program is pretty much a mystery for most people until they approach retirement.

The following five questions test your knowledge of the level and structure of the program's benefits. Don't feel embarrassed if you do not have the faintest idea how to respond to these questions; even most policy analysts cannot come close to providing correct answers.

1. What were the *average* earnings of workers covered by Social Security in 2000? What would the benefits be of a worker who retired in 2000 at age 62 after working steadily for thirty-five years with average lifetime earnings at this level?

    Answer: Average earnings in 2000 were around $32,600. The benefit paid to a worker at age 62 whose earnings placed him or her at the same relative position in the earnings distribution in every year of a thirty-five-year career would be $854 per month.

2. How much would this worker receive if he or she did not apply for benefits at age 62 and kept working at the average wage until age 65?

    Answer: The worker would receive a benefit increased 25 percent to take account of the delay in payment, raising the benefit from $854 per month to $1,066, plus any cost-of-living adjustments that were awarded to retirees.

3. Would Social Security provide a benefit to the individual's spouse even if that spouse had never worked for pay or contributed a penny in payroll taxes?

    Answer: Yes. The spouse would receive a benefit equal to half of the worker's benefit while the worker was alive and equal to the worker's benefit after the worker died.

4. What benefit, if any, would the worker receive if he or she applied for benefits at age 62 but continued to work and earned $25,000 during the next year?

    Answer: The individual's benefit would be cut from $854 per month to $257 per month, but after the worker stopped working when he or she was age 63, the benefit would be permanently increased to approximately $923 a month, plus annual inflation adjustments, for as long as the worker lived. This increase would also extend to widow's benefits for the worker's surviving spouse.

5. A woman marries a man when she is 20 and divorces him when she is 40. When she reaches retirement age, does she receive any pension benefit as a result of that marriage?

    Answer: Yes. If she is not married, she will receive a retirement benefit equal to the larger of the benefit based on her past earnings or 50 percent of the benefit payable to any former spouse to whom she had been married for at least ten years. If she is married, she will receive a benefit based on her past earnings or 50 percent of the benefit payable to her current spouse.

views on how the program should be changed. Although we shall not be bashful about stating those views, we shall do our best to distinguish facts from our own evaluations of those facts. So that you know where we are coming from and where we are heading, the balance of this chapter summarizes our conclusions.

Do We Really Need Mandatory Social Insurance?

Almost without exception, government pension schemes throughout the world force employed workers to pay taxes on their earnings in return for pensions payable when they retire, become disabled, or die leaving dependent children and spouses. Programs under which workers' earmarked tax payments entitle them to future benefits are called "social insurance." Usually, social insurance retirement pensions are provided as annuities—a stream of income paid each year to the retiree and spouse until they die or to the family of the disabled or deceased worker until it is no longer needed.

Everyone understands that it is important for workers to save for retirement and to protect themselves and their dependents against the earnings loss from premature death or disability. But now that most people have some discretionary income, some observers wonder why workers should not decide for themselves how much, when, and in what form to save and to protect themselves and their families from catastrophes. Rather remarkably, almost no one advocates making such saving entirely voluntary. Political liberals, conservatives, and even libertarians recognize that retirement, disability, and survivor pension schemes must be mandatory for two reasons.

Myopia

First, most people would save too little voluntarily to finance retirement or to sustain family income if they became disabled or died prematurely. Most of us find it hard to save. Our reasons—or perhaps excuses—are numerous and often quite imaginative. We tend to regard saving much as St. Augustine regarded virtue when he was young and wild: "Give me chastity and continence," he said, "but not just now." When it comes to saving, people tell themselves they can wait—"until next year," "until the car has been paid off," "until that long-awaited promotion comes through," "until the kids have finished college"—in short, "until later." We must buy now to keep up with, or ahead of, the Joneses or for the pleasures consumption gives us, our children, or our spouses. These satisfactions are tangible, immediate, and real, while our future wants are faint and distant visions in our imagination. Hundreds, if not thousands, of advertisements urge us to buy now—and we do.

In short, saving is hard. If you think this is not your problem, answer the question posed in Box 1–2. That exercise will show why most people need some external restraints to help them resist the temptation to consume more of their income now than is consistent with saving enough to provide for the future.

Unfortunately, the price of putting off saving is high—even exorbitant. Thirty-year-olds have to save 16 percent of their pretax incomes to retire at age 65 with a pension equal to 80 percent of preretirement income. If they wait until crows' feet frame their eyes and gray hairs salt their heads—say, age 45—they would have to stash away a whopping 28 percent of their incomes to reach that same goal.[1]

The lesson is simple: Most people *voluntarily* would save too little and too late to retire at age 65 or even 70 without experiencing a huge drop in their standard of living. Among people age 51 to 61 in 1992, some 25 percent had zero or negative financial net worth, and 75 percent had financial net worth of $36,000 or less. In a 1992 survey nearly half of people age 51 to 61 said that they had thought about retirement "hardly at all" or "only a little."[2] By 2000, the proportion of all workers who said they had saved for retirement had reached 76 percent, but 75 percent of those age 55 or older had saved less than $100,000.[3] In addition, only half of this age group is covered by a private pension, and the benefits from these pensions often will be quite modest. For example, in 1998, more than half of retirees who had any private pension income received less than $6,000 from that source. And so, without mandatory saving through Social Security, retirement at customary living standards would be impossible for most of today's older workers.

BOX 1–2
MYOPIA IN ACTION

Someone offers you the following choice:

YOU CAN HAVE $100 IMMEDIATELY.

or

YOU CAN WAIT FOR A LARGER GUARANTEED PAYMENT ONE MONTH FROM NOW.

What is the smallest amount *payable one month from now* that would cause you to forgo the immediate gift of $100?

WRITE DOWN YOUR ANSWER BEFORE YOU READ ANY FURTHER.

• •

If you are like most people, you will want considerably more than $100—perhaps $125 or even $150—for not taking the very attractive bird-in-the-hand.

Some simple calculations reveal that your request, which you might regard as reasonable, is in fact quite extraordinary. If you said that you would accept $125 in one month, you are implicitly insisting on a 1,355 percent annual rate of return! If you demanded $150, you are saying that you will save $100 for one month only if you receive an annualized rate of return of 12,875 percent! Even if you would accept as little as $110, you would still be demanding what is equivalent to an annual return of 214 percent.

No legal, reasonably safe investment can promise to yield returns anywhere close to 214 percent. Most forms of retirement saving yield somewhere between 3 and 8 percent annually above the inflation rate, which has been running below 3 percent in recent years. This suggests that, if you would have been satisfied with what historically has been a very good rate of return, you should have been willing to accept $100.80 for deferring receipt of the $100 for a month.

This simple example illustrates why, if you are like most people, you will not save enough voluntarily to support yourself adequately in retirement. You may appreciate that you are not really behaving sensibly when you demand such implausibly high returns. That may make you willing to let your employer lock up part of your compensation in a pension plan to which you cannot gain access until you retire. By doing this, you deny yourself the option of succumbing to temptation. But you also acknowledge that, left to your own devices, you would not do what you know is really in your long-term best interest.

MORAL HAZARD

The second reason why all developed nations have made participation in their pension systems mandatory relates to the social "safety nets" they have erected to protect their citizens from destitution. These welfare programs provide insurance against income loss. All types of insurance can cause people to pay less attention to the risks against which they are protected—a response known as "moral hazard." Insured automobile owners can drive with a bit more abandon because insurance pays for damage their recklessness may cause. Homeowners with fire insurance can stint on costly fire-retardant materials when they remodel their homes. Some skiers might take up an orthopedically less hazardous sport or ski fewer black diamond trails if health insurance did not pay for athletic injuries.

In the same way, programs that give income to the destitute may discourage saving, particularly by those who have little hope of saving enough to provide appreciably more than the safety net assures. In fact, they may conclude that it is not worth saving at all. Suppose you knew that you could not possibly save enough to provide appreciably more than $8,520 a year—the approximate value in 2001 of the maximum cash welfare payment for the elderly, the bonus value of food stamps, and the subsidy Medicaid provides to pay the Medicare premiums of the poor elderly. You might well reckon that there is no reason to forgo desirable and necessary consumption during your working years to save for retirement.[4] If many people thought this way, welfare programs for the elderly would cause voluntary retirement saving to fall and the cost of assistance to low-income persons to increase. Benefits available to the indigent disabled or widows create the same problem. Mandatory retirement, survivor, and disability insurance thereby helps people overcome the urge to consume too much when they are young and healthy and also permits more generous aid for the indigent at less cost than would otherwise be possible.

TUNE IT UP OR TRADE IT IN?

Accepting the need for a mandatory system still leaves open the form it should take. The major alternatives now being proposed are partially or fully privatized systems that would shift part or all of the

Social Security payroll tax to personal retirement accounts. Supporters of these approaches advance some powerful arguments. They emphasize the current inadequacy of personal saving and argue that a partially or fully privatized system could boost national saving if it led to larger reserves than those of the current system.[5] If not offset by compensating reductions in other personal or government saving, this source of added national saving would generate increased economic growth that, in turn, could boost tax receipts and help the nation shoulder the future costs of benefits for retiring baby boomers.

Advocates also claim that contributions made to private accounts will earn higher rates of return for workers than would an unchanged Social Security system. If true, lower payroll tax rates would be capable of sustaining any particular level of benefits.

Champions of private accounts also believe that Americans can and should take more responsibility for their own retirement savings. The public is financially more sophisticated than it was in the past. A generation ago, few Americans had invested in anything more complex than a passbook savings account and a fixed-rate mortgage. Now tens of millions own financial assets, but median holdings are modest—$17,500 in stocks, $15,000 in CDs, and $25,000 in mutual funds.[6] Many carry variable-rate mortgages or have refinanced their homes when interest rates have fallen. Millions manage their own personal tax-sheltered savings plans—Individual Retirement Accounts (IRAs)—that supplement Social Security and employer-sponsored pension plans.

While these arguments are appealing, some do not stand up to close scrutiny. Private management, for example, actually lowers rates of return because it is more costly than would be Social Security trust fund management of a similar portfolio. On balance, we conclude that the case for retaining the Social Security system—with certain significant modifications—is stronger. Fundamental to this position is the recognition that Social Security provides greater pension security than could mandatory saving in personal retirement accounts. If the underlying purpose of mandatory saving schemes is to assure retirees, the disabled, and survivors adequate basic incomes, then uncertainty about what that income will be defeats the central objective. The need for reliability leads to two important aspects of Social Security that are not necessarily present in privatized systems.

First, the pension benefit a worker or that worker's dependents receive under Social Security is tied to the worker's earnings over his or her entire career. As a result, the benefit is related to the standard of living to which the worker and dependents are accustomed. Because these average lifetime earnings become increasingly stable as workers approach retirement, benefit levels are known and assured, barring an abrupt legislative change in the benefit formula. Second, the beneficiary must take the pension as an inflation-protected annuity, which ensures that payments will last as long as the pensioner and spouse live and that inflation will not erode the purchasing power of the pension.

In contrast, pensions provided by individual accounts would be uncertain. Even if regulations required the investment of account balances only in broad stock and bond index funds, the resultant pensions would be acutely sensitive to variations in asset prices and interest rates, particularly to variations occurring near a worker's retirement. If workers could select from a wide array of investments for their personal accounts, as they now do with IRAs, the uncertainties would be even larger. A well-established trade-off exists between risk and rates of return. Riskier investments tend to generate higher yields than do safe assets. The only way entirely to escape the risk that asset prices will change is to invest in such options as money-market accounts, which yield less than do assets in which Social Security's reserves are invested. Although millions of Americans have acquired a measure of financial sophistication in managing personal savings, most people know little about finance. Moreover, no degree of financial sophistication can avoid the dilemma that higher-yielding assets are riskier than lower-yielding assets. Even experienced investors sometimes suffer large losses from market gyrations or become victims of cheating and scams. Such reverses are unfortunate for the wealthy. They would be catastrophic for the middle class and poor, particularly if the reverses in financial markets occurred just before retirement, disability, or the death of a breadwinner, because they have few other sources of income to fall back upon.

Furthermore, unless retirees were required to convert their account balances into annuities, some might outlive their retirement savings and end up dependent on welfare assistance. And the purchasing power of these private annuities would be vulnerable to erosion from unanticipated inflation unless they provided inflation protection—which is not yet available in the private annuity market.

While advocates of privatization argue that higher returns would offset such uncertainty, there can be no "Lake Wobegon" effect in the financial market. Unlike Garrison Keillor's mythical Minnesota community where all the children are above average, the average private account cannot enjoy a return much different from the average return on similar investments throughout the economy. But a privatized structure would generate higher sales, administrative, and compliance costs than would Social Security if its reserves were invested in similar assets. Investment management fees would eat into the returns earned by private accounts, diminishing the balances available to support retirement pensions. As a result, the average net returns to pensions on any given portfolio would be higher under Social Security than under direct individual investment, and the pensions would be more reliable. The benefits of earning a higher return can be gained by the Social Security trust funds without imposing uncertainty on individual retirees.

Of course, people should also be encouraged to save voluntarily for retirement and should be free to invest in risky assets. But the income foundation for retirement and disability on which everyone depends should not be subject to the corrosive effects of inflation, interest rate spikes, stock market crashes, or the sharp selling practices that can characterize private financial markets.

Our conclusion is simple. Social Security has worked extremely well and can continue to provide assured basic income support to the retired, the disabled, and families of deceased workers in the future. It equitably spreads across all of society risks that people are ill-equipped to handle individually—such as the possibility that asset prices will collapse, that inflation will accelerate, or that a retiree or retiree's spouse will be blessed with an unusually long life. While Social Security faces genuine financial problems, these problems can and should be solved without changing the fundamental structure of the system. We believe that elected officials and opinion leaders should fix Social Security, not trade it in.

The specific measures that could fix the current system are not complex, but neither will they be widely popular. Privately managed investment of a part of Social Security's reserves in a broad mix of private and public assets would strengthen the program's financial position substantially. The transfer of general revenues to Social Security—a common policy in other nations and one seriously considered when Social Security was crafted in the 1930s—would shift to the general taxpayer part of the pension burden now borne exclusively by workers. But additional measures—benefit cuts or tax increases—are likely to be required to fully address the program's long-run imbalance. In Chapter 6 we outline a program that would not only close the currently projected long-term deficit but also preserve the basic structure of Social Security.

Hanging over the Social Security policy debate is the fact that no one can know for sure what the long-run deficit will turn out to be. This uncertainty has encouraged some experts to prescribe "watchful waiting" as the prudent policy. But uncertainty does not justify procrastination. Implementing changes in Social Security—modifications within the current structure or replacement of part or all of the current system with a new one—will take many years. At the same time, Social Security's deficit might be larger or smaller than current forecasts or might disappear altogether. For this reason, we believe that all modifications in Social Security motivated by financial projections should be introduced gradually.

2

THE CHANGING MEANING
OF RETIREMENT

Shortly before he died in 1995 at the age of 107, the highly successful Broadway impresario George Abbott was asked to recall
the most important change that had come to Broadway during his
long professional life. "Electricity," he replied. Abbott's answer illustrates the staggering transformations that can occur in just one, admit-
tedly very long, life. But numerous equally remarkable changes occur
during lives of more normal durations.

Over the past century, the experience of growing old in America
has changed far more profoundly than any of the transformations
along George Abbott's Great White Way—or in all prior recorded
history. That people now live long enough to share years of retirement
with spouses, children, and grandchildren is unprecedented. Life
expectancies have increased from 47 years for an infant born in 1900
to over 76 years for infants born today. In addition, people can actually afford to retire. Until well into the twentieth century, economic
necessity forced most men to work until they died or physical debil-
ity made work impossible. Financial security in old age and the option
of enjoying years of leisure, health, and independence—once rare
blessings of a privileged few—have become normal and unremark-
able. Most of the credit for this transformation goes to improved
public health, rising incomes, and medical advances, but a good

portion also is attributable to Social Security. Before we turn to a detailed examination of the current policy debate it is instructive to recall what life, work, and growing old was like for generations before Social Security.

A TALE OF FOUR GENERATIONS

A scrim of forgetfulness shields us from a rather ugly picture of what it meant to grow old in America just a couple of generations ago. It is, however, worth drawing back that curtain to look clearly at the harsh realities our forebears faced. Imagine that you are watching, as in time-lapse photography, the lives of people randomly selected from four generations—born in 1860, 1890, 1930, and 1960. The views open in the years in which each group celebrates its twentieth birthday, that is, in 1880, 1910, 1950, and 1980. Watching the experiences of each group unfold helps foster an appreciation of what work and growing old were like for our forebears. It also illustrates what rising incomes, improved public and private health services, and the advent and growth of Social Security and private pensions have meant for everyone—not just for the elderly but also for the disabled, widows, widowers, and their children. It underscores as well the importance of ensuring that, whatever changes the nation makes in its mandatory retirement pension scheme, the accomplishments of the past sixty-five years not be put in jeopardy.

THE 1860 COHORT

This generation was born on the eve of the U.S. Civil War and turned age 20 in the midst of one of America's most rambunctious periods of economic growth and transformation. Its members reached age 60 just after the end of World War I as the Roaring Twenties were getting under way.

A quarter of those born in 1860 had died before reaching age 20. Of those still alive at age 20, nearly half would die before reaching age 65. Living conditions and public sanitation were appalling by today's standards. Infections were common and disease spread quickly. Few houses at the turn of the century had indoor plumbing. Few cities had municipal water and sewer systems. Refrigeration was rudimentary. The books of the muckrakers described the fetid conditions in which food was prepared for the marketplace. Health care was just emerging from the superstition and pretentious ineffectualness that had been its hallmark throughout prior history. Surgery was uncommon and dangerous because surgical technique was primitive and anesthesia was dangerous. Immunization for smallpox was introduced in 1796, but inoculations were uncommon. Children died in droves from childhood diseases, and pneumonia was christened the "widow's friend."

By today's standards, the 1860 cohort would be viewed as a generation of educational dropouts, yet, at that time, America's educational accomplishments led the world. Out of 100 Americans in the 1860 cohort 70 finished primary school, 12 graduated from high school, and three from college.

Average incomes grew remarkably but unevenly between 1880 and 1925. Alternating booms and busts made jobs insecure and retirement saving difficult, even for the thrifty. Thirteen economic contractions, eleven of which lasted more than a year and many of which were catastrophic by modern standards, spotted this 45-year interval. Output fell by more than 7 percent following the 1893 panic and by more than 8 percent in the 1907–08 depression. The economy shrank by about 6 percent on the eve of World War I and by a similar amount after the armistice. Just before the Roaring Twenties got under way, output contracted by more than 13 percent. By contrast, output has fallen no more than 3.7 percent in any of the nine recessions since World War II.

In the course of these fluctuations, America began to urbanize. Nearly three-quarters of the population of 1880 lived on farms or in towns of fewer than 2,500 inhabitants. Only one person in seven lived in one of the 35 cities with more than 50,000 inhabitants. By 1920, fewer than half of the nation's residents lived on farms or in small towns, and close to one-third lived in one of 144 cities with more than 50,000 inhabitants. Nearly half of the population owned their own homes.

Families were large—the average woman gave birth to more than five children. The backbreaking job of caring for children, husbands, brothers, sisters, and parents in a world without washing machines, vacuum cleaners, and dishwashers was a woman's burden, borne until death and lightened only as family members died or moved away. Once married, few white women worked outside the home for pay, although many toiled on the family farm. Those who did work for pay almost invariably performed menial tasks; many, particularly African-American women, were domestics. In the late 1800s, men still filled most of the positions that later would become "women's jobs"—as office secretaries and schoolteachers.

During the early decades of the twentieth century, old age was not a passage to a new mode of living but a continuation of what life was when young. Retirement was a privilege of a wealthy few or a regrettable necessity for the disabled or seriously ill. More than three-quarters of the men still alive when they turned 65 in 1925 continued to work for pay until death, disability, or economic catastrophe intervened.

Such a catastrophe—the Great Depression—did strike when the 1860 cohort was 69 years old. By 1932 almost one-quarter of the labor force was out of work. Older workers were more likely than younger workers to lose their jobs and less likely to find new ones. Protracted unemployment, bank failures, plunging stock market values, and collapsing real estate prices destroyed the savings of those in the middle and working classes who had scrimped and saved for retirement. The millions of newly destitute soon overwhelmed private charities. Public charity dried up, as state and municipal tax collections plummeted. A few older Civil War veterans and their widows and some retired federal workers received small government pensions. Private pensions were rare.

"Retirement" after the economic collapse of 1929 usually meant poverty and dependence on children and other relatives for support. Elderly farmers and their spouses remained on the land, cared for by siblings, children, and in-laws, or they moved to small towns to live with relatives or in group accommodations. In short, the final years were generally pretty grim for the one-third of the 1860 cohort who had survived to celebrate their 69th birthday.

The 1890 Cohort

The 1890 cohort also experienced economic boom and bust. World War I ended a recession and gave some in the class their first taste of foreign travel—albeit in a uniform and under hazardous circumstances. Peace brought another recession, during which the unemployment rate reached nearly 12 percent. After 1921, the good times rolled—except in sectors of squalor, including much of agriculture. Then 1929 ushered in twelve years of economic hell. The Great Depression dried up economic opportunity for this class when it should have been experiencing its peak earning years. Then World War II propelled the United States into frenetic prosperity. Too old to fight again, men from the 1890 cohort helped the home-front economy turn out a limitless arsenal. Women left the home for the paid labor force. No longer confined to what had become the traditional "women's jobs" as secretaries, teachers, social workers, and nurses, they took jobs as machinists and assembly-line operatives, replacing younger men who were island-hopping in the Pacific and debarking on beaches in Africa, Italy, and France. Employers, desperate for workers, discovered that blacks could effectively fill jobs previously denied them by discriminatory taboos. Thus began the great African-American migration from the cotton-belt South to the industrial North. The 1890 cohort experienced the agricultural revolution firsthand. In 1910 when they were 20, some 36 percent of young men worked on farms; by 1950, when the 1890 cohort turned 60, fewer than one in five of the men remained employed in the agricultural sector.

As had been true for earlier generations, the 1890 cohort experienced high rates of infant and childhood mortality, but it benefited from steady, if undramatic, improvements in health and education. Just a little more than one-third of the 20-year-old women and two-fifths of the 20-year-old men in the 1890 cohort did not live to see their 65th birthdays. Four-fifths of this class finished primary school, but only one-fourth graduated from high school, and just 5 percent earned college degrees.

As was the case with the earlier class, only a little more than half of women were living with their spouses when they turned 65. Eighty percent of unmarried elderly women were widows; only 4 percent were divorced. More than three-quarters of 65-year-old men lived with their spouses. Among the unmarried 65-year-old men of 1955, almost half were widowers.

In the mid-1950s when the 1890 cohort turned 65, fewer than half of the elderly had any health insurance, and that coverage was often uncertain because insurers could raise premiums sharply or refuse to renew a policy if the policyholder's health began to deteriorate. But health care expenses were not the financial threat they later became when medical costs soared. Average health care spending of the elderly was less than one-tenth of the current level—only about $660 per year in today's dollars. But the financial threat was serious because health care spending, then as now, was highly concentrated among the few who became seriously ill each year. Those few in the 1890 cohort who lived to their 80s experienced nursing home care— one of the most striking social changes of the second half of the twentieth century. By the late 1970s, nearly one-quarter of the survivors of the 1890 cohort were in nursing homes.

The Advent of Social Security. When the 1890 cohort was in its mid-40s, a revolutionary development occurred—Congress passed the Social Security Act of 1935. It is worth digressing briefly to explain how this upheaval came about and what it involved. When President Roosevelt signed this legislation on August 14, 1935, one-fifth of all workers were unemployed. Fear of job loss was pervasive. The sudden collapse of the freewheeling capitalist system of the Roaring Twenties threatened political instability. Advocates of fringe ideologies such as socialism, communism, and fascism, and peddlers of populist solutions to the nation's economic woes found receptive audiences. Francis Townsend, a California physician, generated widespread support for a wildly irresponsible but attractive plan that promised $200 a month—more than $2,500 a month in today's dollars—to all Americans over age 60 who were not working for pay and agreed to spend it all within a month. Some 3.4 million people joined Townsend's movement. An additional 25 million people signed petitions supporting his plan. At the same time, Governor Huey Long of Louisiana, a charismatic demagogue, gathered wide popular support for his "Share Our Wealth" scheme. It offered a more modest $30 monthly benefit to people over age 60 whose annual incomes were below $1,000 and who owned property worth less than $10,000.[1]

The Social Security Act of 1935, which established not just old-age pensions but also unemployment insurance and several welfare programs, promised both to help ease the economic hardship of the time and to undermine the appeal of political radicals. When enacted, the "old-age insurance" program—the system of contributory pensions for the elderly that is the core of what we now call Social Security—seemed to many a minor element of this landmark legislation. It offered no immediate help to economically hard-pressed older Americans, as the first benefits would not be paid for seven years. Even after 1942, the help that the original Social Security program promised was limited because close to half of all workers—including the self-employed, part-time workers, and workers in agriculture, government, domestic services, and the not-for-profit sectors—were not covered. If the original scope of the program had not been expanded, fewer than one in four of the elderly would have been receiving benefits as late as the mid-1950s when the 1890 cohort turned 65.

The program's anticipated assistance was limited also because benefits were tied to payroll tax contributions made over an entire work life, so that workers would not have retired with full benefits until the mid-1970s.[2] Under this structure, Social Security would have accumulated sizable financial reserves.

It is easy to understand why the public was not overly excited about a program that promised no benefits for seven years, had limited coverage, and offered meager benefits. Other titles of the Social Security Act, such as unemployment insurance and public assistance, delivered immediate assistance to unemployed workers and destitute families. Even the later-reviled Aid to Dependent Children welfare program, which the Social Security Act established, initially enjoyed broader popular support and stronger political backing in Congress than did old-age insurance.[3]

Fortunately for the 1890 cohort, the old-age insurance program was liberalized significantly, first in 1939 and again in 1950. Following the severe economic downturn of 1937, Congress concluded that the lengthy deferral of benefits was unwise. In 1939, it modified the program, initiating pensions in 1940 rather than 1942 and extending benefits to spouses and surviving aged widows and dependents of deceased workers. Coverage was expanded and by 1960 encompassed all workers other than civil servants employed by the federal government or by states and municipalities, or other local governments that chose not to join the program.

Congress also liberalized benefits in 1939 for those who had participated in the program for only a few years, many of whose careers had been blighted by the Great Depression. Workers who retired in 1945 and could have paid payroll taxes for no more than eight years received benefits that averaged $241 a month for single workers and $362 for couples (expressed in 2000 dollars). While these amounts were only about one-third as large as benefits paid today, they were one-fifth and three-quarters larger than those contemplated by the original law.

By boosting benefits, the 1939 law abandoned the policy of building large reserves and adopted "pay-as-you-go" financing, in which current taxes are used to support current benefits and reserve accumulation is scaled back.[4] The decision to forgo reserve accumulation was uncontroversial. Most private and state and local government retirement pension plans held few reserves until the Employee Retirement Income Security Act of 1974 required private pensions to gradually accumulate reserves sufficient to cover past credits.

Social Security and the 1890 Cohort. Even with the introduction and expansion of Social Security, most men of the 1890 cohort kept working to age 65 and beyond. High unemployment and the depressed wages of the Great Depression had blighted the class's prime earning years from age 40 to age 50. Wartime prosperity and the strong economy of the early post-World War II years provided partial compensation. But many still could not afford to retire. Social Security benefits for a couple averaged only about 32 percent of the average earnings of full-time workers, and this benefit was not available to the many who had held noncovered jobs, which, as late as 1949, employed about 40 percent of the workforce. Although one-quarter of all private-sector workers in the 1890 cohort were covered by private pension plans, benefits were usually meager because most had not worked long enough under those pension schemes to receive meaningful benefits.

With insufficient income to retire, two-thirds of surviving men from the 1890 cohort were still working for pay at age 65, nearly half at age 70, and about 30 percent at age 75. In the mid-1950s, more than one-third of those age 65 or older had incomes below official poverty thresholds. Old-age assistance, a welfare program established by the Social Security Act, provided benefits that averaged $323 per month (in 2000 dollars) to 17 percent of the elderly, those who were the poorest and who could not work. In short, even for members of the 1890 cohort, who reached retirement age two decades after the enactment of Social Security, old age was far from a Winnebago holiday.

THE 1930 COHORT

The 2.6 million children born in the depression year of 1930 were just finishing primary school when Japanese dive bombers destroyed the U.S. Pacific fleet at Pearl Harbor, bringing America into World War II. They were on the cusp of adolescence when the war ended and the U.S. economy straightened its shoulders to rebuild a ravaged world. As they turned 20, the cold war turned hot and some were called to fight in the Korean conflict. Between their teens and their mid-40s, the United States economy experienced three decades of rapid growth without major interruption. Real national output per person increased 107 percent, and an avalanche of consumer goods made life at home both easier and more enjoyable.

The 1930 cohort had advantages unavailable to all previous generations. Nearly everyone finished primary school, and seven in ten graduated from high school. In part because of the GI Bill for Korean War veterans, one man in five—but only one woman in nine—graduated from college. Women no longer automatically withdrew from the labor force after they married. Those who left paid work to raise children usually reentered the labor force while still relatively young. Just over one-third worked outside the home when they were age 30, but three-fifths did so when they were age 50. Two-fifths were still working for pay at age 60.

Not all of the 1930 cohort were equally blessed, however. African Americans and Hispanic Americans continued to spend fewer years than whites in school. They studied under poorly trained teachers in inadequately equipped buildings, and attended school with fellow students who performed below grade norm—handicaps that contributed to lifelong economic disadvantage.

If the educational opportunities of the 1930 cohort were striking, the economic achievements were breathtaking. At the start of their working lives, members of the 1930 cohort earned hourly wages three times higher than members of the 1890 cohort had earned in their first jobs. By 1995, when the 1930 cohort turned 65 and left the labor force, their earnings had grown another one-third. The nine recessions that punctuated the post-World War II economic expansion were short and shallow compared with economic paroxysms of the past. Moreover, unemployment compensation cushioned—for up to six months in normal times and even longer during recessions—the economic hardships suffered by those who lost their jobs.[5]

Higher incomes, medical advances, and safer working conditions combined to increase the life expectancy for the 1930 cohort. Two-thirds of the men and over three-quarters of the women born in 1930 lived to celebrate their 65th birthdays. Four-fifths of 65-year-old men and three-fifths of 65-year-old women still lived with a spouse.

As they approached retirement age in the mid-1990s, members of the 1930 cohort had options and resources few of their parents had enjoyed. Most had assets—private pensions or personal savings—that, when combined with Social Security, provided a measure of financial security. Growing numbers of people retired before age 65, particularly after Congress made reduced Social Security benefits available as early as age 62.[6] Nearly one-third of men in the 1930 cohort left the labor force before age 62, two-thirds before age 65. Social Security benefits averaged more than $8,500 yearly for single workers and over $12,000 for couples. After 1974, annual cost-of-living adjustments protected the purchasing power of Social Security benefits. Some of those who were not receiving Social Security benefits at age 65 had chosen to continue working, a decision that would increase their benefits when they did retire. Others were receiving benefits from federal or state and local government pension plans that served as substitutes for Social Security.

By 1995, about one-third of the 1930 cohort received income from a retirement annuity or employment-based pension plan, but the amounts were modest. Half of those with pension income received less than $7,000 a year from this source. When the 1930 cohort reached retirement age, more than four in five owned their own homes and most had benefited from the postwar real estate boom that tripled the real value of owner-occupied housing between 1950 and 1995.

Compared to previous generations, the 1930 cohort also was better protected against soaring medical costs. Medicare, which had been enacted in 1965, provided basic insurance coverage for the elderly and disabled. By the mid-1990s, however, over eight in ten elderly Medicare participants felt the need to supplement this basic coverage with individually purchased Medigap policies or received retiree insurance from former employers or supplemental benefits from Medicaid. Overall, a higher fraction of the 1930 cohort enjoyed health insurance protection than did children and working-age adults, 17 percent of whom lacked insurance coverage.

Average living standards of the elderly by 1995 approximated those of younger adults. Social Security, which provided 42 percent of all cash income of the elderly, was the major force behind this achievement. Only 10.8 percent of the elderly lived in poverty in 1996, a bit less than the 11.4 percent rate of nonelderly adults. Among the elderly, however, major income disparities persisted. While only 4.3 percent of elderly couples were poor in 1996, some 13 percent of elderly single men, 20 percent of all elderly single women, and 36 percent of elderly African-American single women were poor.

The contrast between the 1930 cohort and the earlier classes is striking. Members of the 1930 cohort survived to their 60s in unprecedented proportions. They were able to retire while still fit, and could anticipate a lengthy retirement under living conditions roughly the same as those enjoyed by nonelderly adults.

High poverty rates among aged widows and widowers signal possible economic trouble ahead. Some of the 1930 cohort will run through their assets too quickly. Some couples have private pensions that will terminate when the pensioner dies, leaving survivors with reduced incomes. The purchasing power of most private pensions will erode, as none is adjusted for inflation and few provide increasing payments. Some of the elderly will be forced by chronic infirmity into nursing homes. Others will be overwhelmed by the 45 percent of total health care spending of the elderly that Medicare does not cover. Whatever the future holds for the final years of the 1930 cohort, however, its circumstances represent a revolutionary improvement over those of previous cohorts.

THE 1960 COHORT

The 1960 cohort, born at the tail end of the postwar baby boom, is nearly twice as large as the 1930 cohort. It started off lucky, but with half of its expected life still ahead, we can only speculate about what its old age will be like.

Too young to face combat in Vietnam, America's least popular war, the class took advantage of unmatched educational opportunities. Only one in eight dropped out of high school. Half attended college, and nearly one-fourth—almost as many women as men—earned a bachelor's degree. The fraction of the 1960 cohort with some postcollege education matched the share of the 1860 cohort who completed high school. Eight percent earned a graduate degree. But, as in the past, two groups received less education than the class average. African Americans were only two-thirds as likely as whites to earn a college degree. Barely half of Hispanics completed high school, and only one in ten earned a college degree. These patterns are disturbing because high wages and generous fringe benefits, such as pensions and retiree health benefits, have increasingly become rewards that go to the well-educated worker.

The jobs available to members of the 1960 cohort required less physical strength but more cognitive skills than the positions their parents and grandparents had filled. Nearly three-fifths of men and nearly 90 percent of women in the 1960 cohort work in white-collar or service-sector jobs. Nonetheless, roughly one-quarter of men and a small but growing fraction of women work in physically strenuous occupations such as craftsman, mechanic, miner, machine operator, laborer, or truck driver, jobs that become increasingly difficult to perform as one ages. And tedious work in offices, shops, and factories of the sort that makes one look forward to retirement has not disappeared.

Members of the 1960 cohort were offered significantly higher wages on their first jobs than their parents received when they entered the labor force three decades earlier. But pay rose little until the mid-1990s, particularly for men with less than a college education. Between 1980 and 1996, real full-time earnings of men in this class with no more than a high school diploma grew 57 percent, which was only a bit more than one-third of the earnings increase experienced by similar workers in the 1930 cohort. For those with no more than a high school diploma, one part of the American dream—that sons will earn more than their fathers—may prove to be beyond reach.[7]

The earnings of women in the 1960 cohort are considerably higher than those of previous generations. They are more highly educated, work longer hours, and remain in the paid labor force with fewer interruptions. When they were in their late 30s, roughly 45 percent of the women in the 1930 cohort worked for pay; some 75 percent of the 1960 cohort are holding jobs at that age. Women's earnings have increased significantly faster than those of men. These trends are likely to endure as barriers to women's employment in previously all-male jobs continue to weaken. As a result, many women of the 1960 cohort will be entitled to private pensions, and most will receive Social Security benefits based on their own earnings rather than those of a spouse.

With half of their working lives still ahead, no one knows whether rapid productivity growth or tight labor markets will push up wages and ensure steady employment, or whether low productivity growth and competition from abroad will cause wages to stagnate. Nor can anyone be sure whether most or only a fortunate few will prosper.

Members of the 1960 cohort have told pollsters that they hope to retire earlier than past generations have done, but so far few have saved much. Only 31 percent of those born between 1954 and 1964 have nonhousing assets worth more than $100,000, and 49 percent have accumulated less than $50,000, an amount that would provide a couple at age 65 with an annuity of less than $4,000 a year. Unlike their parents, members of the 1960 cohort are unlikely to enjoy the windfall of a protracted real estate boom. Easy credit from home equity loans, automobile loans, and proliferating credit cards will continue to encourage consumption and discourage saving.

In their failure to save, members of the 1960 cohort are no different from their forebears, who began to save, if at all, only in their late 40s and 50s. When they reach that age, however, the 1960 cohort may find it harder to put something aside to make up for youthful fecklessness. They are marrying late and deferring child bearing. As a result, many will be well into their 50s before their children have finished school and moved away. Furthermore, if current trends hold, about half of all the first marriages of the cohort will end in divorce, an event that disrupts both family life and retirement saving. Most who divorce will remarry, but about one-third will find themselves single at age 65, not because they were widowed—the fate of three-quarters of single 65-year-olds in the 1860 cohort—but because two out of five will be divorced.

On the bright side, more members of the 1960 cohort than of previous generations should receive sizable private pension benefits when they retire. Although the fraction of workers covered by employment-related plans has not increased in two decades, the fraction of workers who will actually receive sizable pensions will grow. One reason is the requirement contained in the Employee Retirement Income Security Act of 1974 that pension rights vest in no more than five years. Furthermore, the Pension Benefit Guarantee Corporation now ensures that the basic benefits promised by company-managed, defined-benefit pension plans will be paid even if the sponsoring company goes broke.

At the same time, pensions are becoming increasingly vulnerable to financial market volatility. Plans that pay benefits until the worker dies, based on the worker's earnings and number of years of service— traditional "defined-benefit" plans—are giving way to "defined-contribution" and "cash balance" plans in which the pension depends on the amounts contributed to the account and the investment returns earned on those contributions. The proportion of private-sector workers covered by private pensions whose primary plan was defined-benefit fell from 87 percent in 1975 to 56 percent in 1997. Benefit adequacy under defined-contribution plans depends on what happens to asset prices and on how long the retiree and spouse live. If the balances accumulated in the defined-contribution plan are not used to buy an annuity upon retirement, which for reasons we discuss in Chapter 5 can be a fairly expensive undertaking, many retired workers or their spouses will outlive their retirement pensions. Half of the men in the 1960 cohort who reach age 65 are projected to still be alive at age 83, and more than one-fifth will live to their 90th birthdays in 2050. Of women who live to age 65, half will still be alive at age 87. Medical advances could easily raise these fractions.

If current trends continue, half of the men in the 1960 cohort will retire by age 62 and half of the women by age 60. They will face a prospect that was virtually unknown to their great-great-grandparents in the 1860 cohort—a quarter-century or more of retirement. New patterns, however, may emerge. Members of the 1960 cohort may choose to retire later or more gradually than in the past. They may leave the jobs that sustained them in their primary earning years and move into less demanding positions. Or they may choose to work part-time or part-year. The rapid growth in part-time jobs and the development of contract and contingent work have already created many such opportunities. Labor force growth is projected to slow to only 0.3 percent a year—one-quarter its current rate—by the time the 1960 cohort is in its 60s. Tight labor markets could encourage employers to make special efforts to accommodate the preferences and needs of older workers. The remarkable flexibility of the American workplace ensures further changes in response to market pressures.

WHAT LIES AHEAD?

Public policy will help determine whether long retirements, even if desirable, are affordable. Even if the wage growth of the late 1990s is sustained, few of today's young workers are likely to have enough personal saving or private pension benefits to support themselves in comfort for a quarter of a century in retirement. Like the current generation of elderly, they will be highly dependent on Social Security or its alternative.

If the Social Security program's projected long-term deficit materializes, some cutback in benefits or increase in revenues will be inescapable. The structure that has developed over the past six decades could be reinforced and modified to reflect the changes that have taken place in the nation's economic, social, and demographic character since 1935. Small adjustments along these lines made soon and phased in gradually would be enough to do the job. Or the current structure could be gradually transformed into one in which individual retirement accounts play a significant role. In that case, the risks inherent in long-term pension contracts, which are now shared collectively, would be placed directly on individuals. How and when these decisions are made will shape the economic terms on which members of the 1960 cohort—and those who follow them—grow old and retire.

3

KEY ISSUES IN THE SOCIAL SECURITY DEBATE

The current Social Security debate centers on two contrasting positions. One holds that Social Security, with some reforms, represents the best way to guarantee basic income protection for retirees, the disabled, and survivors. The other maintains that mandatory saving through individual accounts would be more effective. Although the issues seem complex and the rhetoric often confusing, the debate boils down to three questions.

◆ *How Should Benefits Be Set?* Should pensions be based on what participants have earned and how long they have worked—which is how defined-benefit plans are structured—or on the amounts workers and their employers have contributed to retirement accounts and the investment returns earned on those contributions—which is how defined-contribution plans work?

◆ *How Much Social Assistance?* Should the nation's basic pension program provide benefits proportional to earnings or to contributions and investment returns on contributions, or should benefits be boosted for low earners, widowed spouses, and others who might be regarded as deserving or vulnerable? In short, how much "social" should there be in social insurance?

◆ *How Much Reserve Accumulation?* Should the pension plan build reserves? If so, who should pay the added costs of building up those reserves, and who should manage the investment of those reserves?

HOW SHOULD BENEFITS BE SET?

Pension contracts can span 70 or more years—the time between a worker's first payroll tax payment and the last pension check paid to the worker or to a surviving spouse. Promises that span so many years are inescapably risky. The extent to which these risks should be reflected in individuals' benefits—in other words, the question of who should bear the risks—is a central issue in the debate about how social insurance should be designed. Defined-benefit plans, such as Social Security, distribute those risks differently from the defined-contribution plans that have been proposed as full or partial replacements of the existing system.

One class of risks—"system" risks—relates to maintaining the pension system's financial balance. If the system gets out of kilter, whose benefits or taxes should be changed? Even if the overall system remains in financial balance, individuals face another class of risks—"personal" risks from unemployment, low earnings, low investment returns, sickness, and changing family situations—in short, from developments over which workers have only limited control. Personal risks increase when workers can select a pension plan administrator, choose the assets in which their contributions are invested, or decide whether to take their pensions as lump-sum withdrawals, annuities, or scheduled payments. In each case, good or lucky decisions can increase pension returns, but bad or unlucky decisions can lower them.

SYSTEM RISKS

Because pension contracts run for so many years, they inevitably get out of balance. Unanticipated economic and demographic developments cause revenues and outlays to differ from expectations. The imbalances take different forms under defined-benefit and defined-contribution plans but are as likely under one type of plan as under the other.

When confronted with imbalances in Social Security, which is a defined-benefit program, Congress has typically modified benefits for current and future pensioners and changed tax rates, thus spreading the adjustments broadly across many people and years. In 1972, for example, when improved methods of estimating future revenues and costs revealed large projected surpluses, Congress responded by raising benefits, mostly for future retirees. When faced with the cumulative impact of the unexpected slowdown in productivity growth after 1973, recessions in the mid-1970s and early 1980s, and a flaw in the 1972 legislation that raised benefits excessively, Congress responded by cutting benefits for current and future retirees in various ways and by raising taxes (see Box 3–1, page 34, for details of legislation enacted in 1983).

Under defined-contribution plans, pensions can not exceed the balance in an individual's account at the time of retirement. Imbalances show up as pensions that are larger or smaller than those that were planned. Variations in the growth of average earnings or in the returns on investments can create such imbalances.[1] The only way to deal with such imbalances under a defined-contribution plan is periodically to change contribution rates. Such changes can restore intended pension levels for young and even middle-aged workers—provided that further disturbances do not occur as workers near retirement. But there is no effective way to correct imbalances that occur shortly before workers reach retirement age. If asset prices drop when a worker is, say, age 64, there is no practical way to restore pensions to their intended levels because changes in contribution rates add only slowly to balances. In such cases, workers are simply stuck with lower benefits. In short, the consequences of correcting—or not correcting—imbalances in a defined-contribution pension system for any worker fall entirely on that worker.

Routine fluctuations in asset values, interest rates, and wage growth make it likely that defined-contribution pensions will not produce intended replacement rates—the ratio of pensions to prior earnings—unless contribution rates are changed frequently and by large amounts. Figure 3–1 (see page 35) shows how replacement rates would have varied if an average male worker invested a constant fraction of his earnings in a "total stock market" index fund during his working years and converted the balance at age 62 into an annuity.[2] In this example, workers reaching retirement age in the years between

---

BOX 3–1
SPREADING THE RISK—HOW CONGRESS
CLOSED THE DEFICIT IN 1983

In 1972, Congress enacted a formula to adjust Social Security benefits automatically for wage inflation. Unfortunately, the adjustments were too large and a deficit emerged. Congress enacted legislation in 1977 to correct the formula and close the deficit, but deficits continued because slow economic growth persisted, inflation accelerated over the 1979–81 period, and unemployment soared during the recessions of 1980 and 1981–82.

Soon after taking office, President Reagan proposed major benefit cuts to close the Social Security deficit. His proposed changes proved quite unpopular. To limit political damage, he appointed a commission under the chairmanship of economist Alan Greenspan to design a plan to restore balance. The proposals of this commission were the basis of the legislation enacted in early 1983, only months before the reserves in the trust funds would have been depleted.

The changes, which dealt with both the short-run, cash-flow problem and the long-run deficit, affected current workers and beneficiaries as well as future beneficiaries. A previously scheduled increase in the payroll tax was accelerated. All employees of nonprofit organizations and new federal government employees were brought under Social Security. Since most of these workers earned eligibility through private employment before, during, or after their current jobs, this change raised revenues far more than costs. A portion of the benefits received by upper-income recipients was subject to the personal income tax, and the resulting revenues were returned to the trust funds. The revenues from this change were projected to grow significantly because the income thresholds at which the provision became effective were not adjusted for inflation. The cost-of-living adjustment for benefits was suspended for six months, permanently lowering benefits for all current beneficiaries. The tax rate on the self-employed, previously three-fourths of the combined rate on employees and employers, was raised to parity. Smaller changes affecting other groups were also made.

1911 and 1999 would have had replacement rates that ranged from 18.2 percent of earnings to 100.2 percent of earnings, depending on the year in which they reached retirement age. Furthermore, because price increases continue even after workers convert their savings to annuities, and private markets do not yet offer indexed annuities, the purchasing power of pensions typically declines as each worker ages. During periods of relatively rapid inflation, the loss can be severe. For example, workers who turned age 70 during the period from 1965 through 1975 saw the real value of their pensions drop as much as half over the ensuing decade.

FIGURE 3–1

MALE SINGLE-LIFE ANNUITY AS A PERCENTAGE OF CAREER
HIGH ANNUAL EARNINGS (MEASURED AT AGE 62)

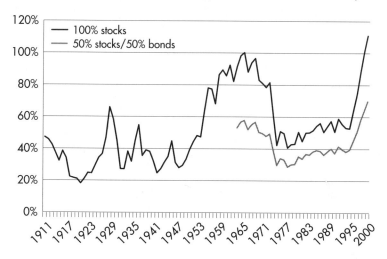

Notes: Economywide real wage growth = 2 percent; contribution rate = 6 percent; forty-year career; invest in stocks over forty-year career; convert to level annuity at age 62.

Source: Unpublished figure prepared by Gary Burtless, The Brookings Institution.

Figure 3–1 correctly indicates the *variability from one year to another* of pensions invested exclusively in common stocks, but it omits certain risks. First, it ignores variability in pensions that would arise from changes in stock values that occur *within* a given year. As experiences in 1987 and 2000 illustrate, these differences can be large. Workers who sold their holdings at the market close on October 19, 1987, would have realized 18 percent less than workers who sold the day before. Workers who invested in an index of stocks listed in the Standard and Poor's 500 or the NASDAQ who sold their holdings at year end 2000 would have realized 13.6 percent and 51.1 percent less than if they had sold their holdings when these indexes were at their peaks early in 2000.

Second, if workers are free to pursue different investment strategies, they will realize widely varying pensions, even if they are the same age, make the same contributions each year, and convert their holdings into annuities on the same date. Because many investors would not choose a total stock market index fund but instead would choose to hold a different mix of stocks or a mix of stocks and bonds, the variation in returns *over time* would differ from that shown in Figure 3–1. Pension reserves invested in long-term bonds are subject to price fluctuations similar to, but smaller than, those of stocks. If bonds are held to maturity, unexpected inflation affects the real value of the account balance. Increased inflation can cause the price of long-term bonds sold before maturity to fall precipitously. In 1982, for example, a thirty-year AT&T bond issued in 1977 was worth only 35 percent as much (adjusted for inflation) as it was at issue five years earlier. Finally, the actual *level* of replacement rates would be considerably lower than those shown in Figure 3–1 because the calculations depicted there ignore costs of managing funds during the accumulation period and of annuitization and payout, which can sharply reduce the growth of balances.

Variations in asset prices do not directly affect workers' pensions under defined-benefit plans because pensions are based on workers' earnings. Fluctuations in asset prices and interest rates can indirectly affect benefits and taxes under defined-benefit systems. A permanent drop in asset values, for example, would eventually require either benefit cuts or tax increases, if one wanted to keep a system continually in precise balance. The effects, however, are surprisingly small. Suppose that projected revenues and benefits over the next seventy-five years were in balance and that reserves equal to ten times annual benefit payments were invested equally in stocks and government securities. A 30 percent drop in stock prices would produce a deficit equal to less than 2.5 percent of long-term benefits or revenues. If projected revenues initially equaled projected outlays, such a shock would not be sufficient to push the Social Security system out of "close actuarial balance," defined by the Social Security actuaries as any situation in which projected revenues are between 95 percent and 105 percent of projected outlays. In contrast, under a defined-contribution pension, such a drop in stock prices would reduce the value of a similarly invested individual account by 15 percent. The pension of a worker reaching retirement when the shock occurred would be reduced by the same amount, six times more than the reduction under a defined-benefit plan such as Social Security if balance were restored exclusively through benefit cuts.

To be sure, workers or pension fund managers can protect themselves from price volatility under defined-contribution plans by shifting from stocks and long-term bonds to short-term bonds and money-market instruments. But this strategy sacrifices expected earnings. The prices of money-market funds and short-term Treasury securities are stable, but long-term yields on these securities have barely exceeded inflation. In contrast, annual returns on common stocks have greatly exceeded inflation—by an average of 8.3 percent in the forty years from 1960 through 1999, and by 13.6 percent in the twenty years since 1980.

INDIVIDUAL RISKS

Even if a plan remains in overall balance, the pensions of individual workers are subject to risk. Both defined-benefit and defined-contribution pensions depend on how much workers earn. Defined-contribution pensions are also sensitive to the timing of earnings, which can be affected by myriad unanticipated events—involuntary unemployment, a job change, poor health, or the birth of a child, for example. Early career earnings count more than do later career earnings, because early pension fund contributions have a longer time to earn interest or enjoy stock price increases than do later contributions.[3]

Social Security's benefits are determined by workers' earnings averaged over their working lives (see Box 3–2, page 40). Those whose earnings averaged over the thirty-five years of highest earnings are the same, receive the same pensions, whether earnings were relatively high or low at the beginning of a worker's career or whether, for one reason or another, the worker had no earnings in some years.

An additional element of individual risk—and opportunity—is introduced if participants are given some control over how their accounts' reserves are invested, as is the case with most defined-contribution plans. Social Security offers no choice. Under current law, reserves must be invested in secure, but low-yielding, U.S. government securities. Some proposals to strengthen the Social Security system or to establish individual accounts would shift a portion of the reserves to higher-yielding stocks and corporate bonds. Some individual account plans would limit investments to a few index funds or to a single, blended stock and bond fund. Others would permit workers to choose among a wide range of assets. The greater the range of

> ## BOX 3–2
> ## FIGURING OUT YOUR AVERAGE EARNINGS
>
> Social Security benefits are based on a worker's earnings averaged over the 35 years in which the worker's *adjusted* earnings are highest. A simple example illustrates the calculation.
>
> Suppose you worked every year from age 22 through age 61, a forty-year period. The first step would be to adjust your past earnings to reflect the increase in economy-wide average earnings between the year you received the earnings and the year you turned age 60. For example, if you turned 62 in 2000, your 1960 earnings would be multiplied by 7.2 for averaging purposes because that is how much average wages increased between 1960 and 1998, the year in which you turned 60. If you earned $4,000 in 1960, that would be transformed into earnings of $28,800 to calculate your average earnings. A similar adjustment would be made for your earnings in each of the other thirty-nine years you worked. The second step would be to select the highest thirty-five of your forty years of adjusted earnings. The third step would be to calculate the average of these adjusted earnings.
>
> Under this procedure, the importance of each dollar of earnings is adjusted by the growth of economy-wide earnings between the year the earnings were received and the year the worker turns age 60. In contrast, the importance of each dollar contributed to a defined-contribution pension plan grows at the rate earned by the plan's investments. Early earnings count more heavily under a defined-contribution plan than under Social Security if the investment return exceeds the growth rate of earnings per worker. Historically, this has been the case, and the Social Security Administration projects a similar pattern for the future. The projections suggest that the real interest rate on government securities will average 3.0 percent, while real earnings per worker will grow 1 percent annually. If history is any guide, real returns on private equities will be two or three times that on government securities.
>
> Under such assumptions, the loss of earnings early in one's career will reduce one's lifetime pension in a defined-contribution system proportionately more than it will under Social Security. In contrast, early retirement will reduce pensions proportionately more under Social Security than under a defined-contribution system. There is an important exception to this general rule. If one becomes disabled under a defined-contribution plan, payments into one's pension fund cease. Social Security contains a "disability freeze," which means that if one becomes disabled, the number of years of earnings counted in computing retirement benefits is reduced to take account of the shortened working life. As a result, the Social Security retirement benefits that a disabled worker eventually receives are not affected by the years of zero earnings after the onset of disability.

choice open to workers, the greater the variation there will be in pensions different workers with the same earnings receive. Even if workers were limited to a single total stock market fund, however, the variation over time would be considerable, as shown in Figure 3–1.

With wider choices, some workers would make good investment choices and earn very high returns, while others would make bad investment decisions and earn very low returns or even lose part of their initial investments. Even highly conservative investment strategies can backfire. Investors who purchased seemingly safe stocks like the Pennsylvania and New York Central railroads in the 1950s discovered they were holding worthless certificates when the merged company—the Penn Central—declared bankruptcy in 1970. Investors who took a flyer on unknown startup companies like Intel or Microsoft could retire rich, but others who sank their retirement nest eggs into other new companies that did poorly or went bankrupt would have experienced returns well below average or lost their investments altogether.

Uncertainties and risks do not end with retirement. The same market risks would continue for workers who do not buy annuities or who buy annuities whose value depends on stock prices—so-called variable annuities. Workers who do not buy annuities run the risk that they may exhaust their accumulated retirement savings years before they die. And unexpected inflation threatens those who buy annuities; they face the steady erosion in the purchasing power of pensions, which may have seemed adequate at first.

All Social Security retirement benefits are inflation-protected annuities. The defined-contribution components of most of the plans proposed as replacements to Social Security would allow retirees to withdraw their retirement savings as lump sums or transfer them to heirs, as periodic payments over a fixed time period or as annuities. Few require that pensions take the form of indexed annuities.

The importance of protecting basic retirement income from inflation cannot be exaggerated. Mortality rates are falling fast. The Census Bureau forecasts that by 2050 there will be more than 31 million people over age 80 and 1 million centenarians. The longer people live, the greater the damage that inflation can do to pensions that are not protected from erosion by inflation. An inflation rate of 2.5 percent—the Congressional Budget Office's long-term projection for inflation—will cut the purchasing power of an unindexed pension by 43 percent by the time a 62-year-old reaches age 85.

People who must deal financially with the uncertainty of how long they might live face two unsatisfactory options. They may spend their retirement savings very slowly, minimizing the risk that they will outlive their savings but increasing the possibility that they will die having deprived themselves unnecessarily of consumption they could have afforded. Or they may spend their resources quickly, minimizing the chance that they will deprive themselves needlessly, but risking destitution and dependency on relatives or public charity at the end of their lives.

Although annuities—an income stream guaranteed to last as long as the pensioner lives, but not longer—provide a simple way out of this dilemma, few people buy them. One reason is cost. Insurance companies have found that people who expect to live a long time are more likely to buy annuities than people with short life expectancies. Those who are terminally ill or whose parents and grandparents did not live much beyond their 60s are less likely to buy an annuity than those who are healthy and whose forebears lived into their 90s. As a result of such "adverse selection," insurance companies charge about 10 percent more for annuities than they would if the average purchaser had a normal life expectancy. Selling and administrative costs boost prices roughly 10 percent more. In total, annuity buyers with average life expectancy might easily give up about 20 percent of the value of the assets they convert into an annuity. Prices vary significantly by company, so that some people pay more and some pay less (see Box 3–3).

In principle, insurance companies could ask for information that would let them estimate how long each annuity purchaser might live and charge those with shorter life expectancies less than others. Such information would be imperfect at best. Furthermore, legal restrictions limit such price discrimination. In practice, insurance companies charge people of the same age and sex the same price for an annuity.[4]

Insurance companies have been unwilling to offer private annuities that entirely eliminate the risk. Until recently, no inflation-indexed securities were available to reduce their risk.[5] Bonds have not filled the need because their yields have proven to be poor indicators of future inflation. During the two decades from 1976 through 1996, the forecast of inflation over the succeeding ten years implicit in bond prices differed from actual inflation by more than 50 percent in most years in U.S., British, and Japanese financial markets.[6] Although the government now issues long-term, inflation-indexed bonds that could be used to back inflation-protected annuities, a market has yet to emerge for such a product. Annuity purchasers

BOX 3–3
THE PRICE OF ANNUITIES

The annual payout that insurance companies offer 65-year-old men in return for a $100,000 annuity varies widely.[a]

| | | RATE OF RETURN AS PERCENTAGE OF YIELD ON | |
	ANNUAL PAYOUT	TREASURY BONDS	CORPORATE BONDS
Average company	$9,528	82	74
Ten highest-payout companies	10,464	90	82
Ten lowest-payout companies	8,700	75	68

The average annuity provides a rate of return 26 percent lower than a 65-year-old man would realize on corporate bonds if he lived exactly the average life expectancy of 65-year-old men. About 10 percentage points of this differential arise because those who buy annuities live longer than average. The remainder arise because companies selling annuities have marketing and administrative costs and must earn a profit. Because individual companies have different cost structures, have different expectations about how much they can earn on their investments, and may sell to groups with different life expectancies, there is wide variation among companies in their payout rates.

Whatever the source of the differential, two facts are clear. First, a man who purchases an annuity is giving up 18 to 32 percent of the return he could earn if he invested directly in a corporate bond fund (essentially similar conclusions apply to women). To be sure, the purchaser gets something valuable in return—the assurance that the payment will last as long as he lives. Under certain assumptions this insurance may be worth the cost charged by the *average* insurance company.

The second fact is that it pays to shop around. The top-payout companies offer 17 percent more than the bottom-payout companies. The value of insurance against outliving one's assets easily offsets the extra charges of the highest payout companies. But unless people are unusually worried about outliving their assets, most will be better off "self-insuring"—investing conservatively and spending gradually—than buying annuities from the lowest-payout companies.

---

a. Olivia S. Mitchell, James M. Poterba, and Mark J. Warshawsky, "New Evidence on the Money's Worth of Individual Annuities," NBER Working Paper no. 6002, National Bureau of Economic Research, Cambridge, Mass., April 1997.

seem reluctant to accept a real rate of interest of about 3.75 percent—less insurance companies' commissions, other administrative costs, and profits—which is what this protection would entail.

HOW MUCH SOCIAL ASSISTANCE?

Social Security has always provided more generous benefits, relative to earnings or past payroll tax contributions, to some participants than to others. The big gainers are low earners. For example, although $35,000 earners pay half the payroll taxes of $70,000 earners, they receive pensions that are only 29 percent smaller.

Benefits also are higher for couples and families than for single beneficiaries. Social Security provides benefits to elderly spouses equal to half of the retired worker's benefit if the spouse has had no or only a limited work history. When the retired worker dies, the surviving spouse's benefit is raised to the level of the deceased worker's benefit. If the retired worker has dependent children, Social Security also provides a benefit for them.[7] Similar benefits are provided to survivors when a worker becomes disabled or dies before reaching the retirement age.

Social Security benefits for surviving spouses and children of deceased workers and retirees comprise a kind of life insurance that is paid out in monthly installments, rather than as a lump sum. The estimated value of this life insurance for active workers in 2000 was $13–14 trillion. Such benefits and the pensions paid to retired workers' spouses with limited work histories clearly have more value to married than to single workers and more importance to families with children than to the childless. Nevertheless, married workers and those with large families pay the same payroll tax rate on their earnings as single workers with no spouses or children.

Taken together, these provisions reduce the likelihood that low earners, couples, and surviving spouses and dependent children will be poor. In fact, Social Security keeps twice as many people out of poverty as do all of the government's cash and in-kind welfare programs. That Social Security protects workers against low earnings as well as disability and death of a breadwinner means that the total return workers receive for their payroll taxes is higher than the financial return as measured by the actual pension benefits. People willingly buy term life insurance or fire insurance although they hope never to collect anything and the expected cash payouts are smaller than the premiums they pay. Such insurance is attractive because people prize protection from large risks they wish to avoid. The value of similar protections against the risks of disability, death, or low earnings that Social Security provides should be added to the actual pension payments in computing its total economic return.

MAKING DEFINED-CONTRIBUTION PLANS PROGRESSIVE

In their pure form, defined-contribution pension plans do not provide assistance to low earners or to other vulnerable groups. The payout is simply the amounts contributed, plus accumulated earnings, as with any savings plan. But certain modifications can add such assistance.

Subsidies. Direct subsidies can be provided to low earners. For example, the USA account plan proposed in 1999 by President Clinton offered refundable tax credits to families whose incomes fell below stipulated thresholds if they made deposits to qualified accounts. Inequities would occur if subsidies were based on individual workers' earnings because some low earners are not members of low-income households. And even if subsidies are based on family income, some families with low incomes in one year will become wealthy in the future or were high earners in the past. Unintended subsidies can be reduced but not without adding considerable complexity to the system. For example, the government subsidy could be based on earnings or on earnings plus capital income averaged over a worker's lifetime.

Hybrid Plans. A defined-contribution pension plan can be paired with a defined-benefit plan. The defined-benefit plan can support low earners and spouses with limited work histories, for example, by providing all retirees an inflation-protected flat benefit related to the number of years worked plus a spouse's benefit. The defined-contribution plan could supplement the flat benefit.[8]

Hybrid plans can be designed to achieve whatever degree of income protection society deems appropriate. Whether such a plan could be enacted and sustained is less clear. Social Security has forged a political alliance between high and moderate earners who receive sizable pensions and low earners who receive social assistance. Splitting pensions and social assistance into separate programs would break this alliance. Over time, such a separation could weaken public support for assistance to low earners, spouses with limited work histories, and dependent family members.

Income-tested Assistance. Social assistance for survivors and the elderly poor also can come through income-tested programs. Were

Social Security replaced in whole or in part with individual accounts that provide no social assistance, income- or means-tested programs could be expanded. Unfortunately, income and means tests are costly to administer, adding as much as 10 percent to total program costs. In the United States, income- and means-tested programs typically carry a stigma that deters some people who are legally entitled to benefits from claiming them, a serious disadvantage in a benefit intended to be universal.

A SUMMING UP

Social Security has never been known primarily as a program to fight poverty or to provide aid to families with children. Nonetheless, it has become the federal government's most important antipoverty and family support program. Through this social assistance, it has contributed significantly to the reduction of poverty among all age groups. Furthermore, this assistance has been provided without the stigma of means tests. Any shift to a defined-contribution system will make it more difficult and controversial to sustain such assistance, as it would be cumbersome to administer and vulnerable to political attack.

HOW MUCH RESERVE ACCUMULATION?

Up to the present, elected officials in the United States and most other developed countries have preferred pay-as-you-go financing. The reason is simple—building large reserves requires legislatures either to keep benefits small for several decades after a plan's inception or to set taxes high enough both to pay significant benefits to those retiring in the program's early decades and to build reserves. Initial Social Security pensions, although modest, far exceeded what the average beneficiary's payroll tax contributions justified. For example, the group that turned 65 between 1950 and 1955 received benefits that were almost four times higher than their past contributions warranted.

Pay-as-you-go financing also operates on the principle that funds contributed by younger workers pay for benefits for retired workers.

Some deride such financing as a Ponzi or pyramid scheme, similar to the scam Charles Ponzi developed in the 1920s. He used funds gathered from later depositors to pay high returns to early depositors (see Box 3–4, page 46). When doubts about the scheme's viability arose, new deposits dried up. The scheme collapsed. Depositors cried foul. And Ponzi went to prison.

The analogy of pay-as-you-go Social Security to Ponzi's fraud is flawed in two crucial respects: Ponzi promised larger returns than any plausible growth of his "customer base" could sustain, and his system was *voluntary*. If Social Security promised benefits that grew much faster than the nation's economy, it too would be unsustainable. But pay-as-you-go social insurance can permanently provide a return on contributions equal to the rate of growth of total earnings—the sum of the growth of the workforce and of earnings per worker (see Box 3–5, page 47). Similarly, if Social Security were voluntary—for example, if participation were voluntary and high-income wage earners and those who felt they could do better saving privately opted out of the system—it would soon collapse (see Box 3–6, page 48, for an explanation of why voluntary Social Security cannot work). But Social Security is mandatory. By keeping returns reasonable and participation mandatory, Social Security can proceed indefinitely on a pay-as-you-go basis.

In fact, Social Security is now run on a partially funded basis. Approximately $3 of every $4 of Social Security income now goes to pay current benefits.[9] The remaining $1 is invested in U.S. government securities. In 2000, Social Security revenues exceeded expenditures by more than $155 billion. Reserves at year-end were a bit more than $1 trillion. Annual surpluses are projected to exceed $260 billion in 2010, and total reserves are projected to reach a maximum of some $6 trillion in 2024. These figures are impressive but not nearly as large as they would be if the system were fully funded.

Workers receive a real (inflation-adjusted) return on their payroll taxes that is a blend of the pay-as-you-go return, currently about 1 percent, and the yield on government securities, projected to average 3 percent.[10] To the extent that the benefit formula promises to provide workers in the *future* with a higher return on their taxes than this blended rate, current workers will have to pay more in taxes, accept lower benefits, or receive higher returns on trust fund investments.

BOX 3–4
THE COLORFUL LIFE OF CHARLES PONZI

Charles Ponzi's profession is listed in the *Biographical Almanac* as "swindler." Ponzi's name is immortal because he had the genius to turn a legitimate business venture into a very lucrative crime.

A native of Italy, Ponzi began his life of crime early, stealing from his parents and parish priests. He emigrated to Canada and then to the United States, where additional petty crimes led to short jail sentences. In 1919, he discovered "arbitrage"—making money by buying the same asset in one market and selling it at a higher price in another market. The asset was postage stamps. The International Postal Union sold certificates that could be used in post offices of various nations to purchase sufficient postage to send letters internationally. The cost of such certificates in Spain was 1 cent. The certificate was good for 5 cents worth of postage in the United States. This is the same sort of transaction in which "arbitrageurs" engage, buying grain, currency, or other materials in one market and selling it in another where prices are higher. Such transactions, which tend to raise prices in the low-price market and lower them in the high-price market, are entirely legitimate.

Ponzi had an innovation—he lied. After explaining the transaction to gullible investors, he neglected to inform them that he really had no way to convert the U.S. stamps back to cash. He also failed to tell them that he was not buying postal certificates at all. Instead, he simply kept what initial investors paid him and, as more money rolled in, he repaid the initial investors, never failing to skim funds for himself. Ponzi did very nicely, collecting "investments" worth $154 million in 1996 dollars.[a] He bought a twenty-room mansion and a bank, and in general lived very well. Eventually, he made a very serious blunder. He hired a public relations expert to help him maintain his image, an *honest* public relations expert, who quickly recognized fraud and reported it to the authorities. Ponzi ended up in prison, from which he wrote letters to former investors expressing regret that he could not help them but promising to do so as soon as he got out. The immigration authorities had other plans, however, deporting Ponzi to his native Italy. With few resources, he joined Mussolini's fascist movement and became a high ranking treasury official, until his incompetence was discovered. At that point, he was sent to Brazil as manager of the new national airline Alitalia. Following the war and Mussolini's death, Ponzi lost his job and his money. He died penniless, tended only by a nun.

Frauds that closely resemble Ponzi's scheme abound. Everyone seems susceptible. One-sixth of the citizens of Romania fell for a Ponzi scheme in 1993. Nearer to home, the celebrated Foundation for New Era Philanthropy, a scheme that promised to double and triple the gifts wealthy donors wanted to give to charity, gulled people as sophisticated as William Simon, former Treasury Department secretary; John Whitehead, former managing partner of the investment firm, Goldman, Sachs; and Laurence Rockefeller, financier.

---

[a] David Segal, "Money for Nothing: Forget the Work Ethic; Mr. Ponzi Showed Us the Real American Dream," *Washington Post,* June 2, 1996, Outlook section, p. 1.

BOX 3–5
WHAT RETURN CAN PAY-AS-YOU-GO
SOCIAL INSURANCE PAY?

The average real rate of return on payroll tax payments equals the growth of real earnings, which in turn equals the growth of employment multiplied by the growth of output per worker.

This is the fundamental proposition of pay-as-you-go social insurance. The following examples illustrate this proposition. Suppose that people's adult lives are divided into two periods. They work for the first period and collect pensions in the second. Assume further that N people comprise each cohort or age group. Each worker earns E. Both population and earnings are stable. The payroll tax rate is t. That means that each worker pays taxes of tE and tax collections from each cohort are tEN.

Under pay-as-you-go financing, all taxes are paid out as benefits to the N members of the older cohort. Benefits per retiree equal total tax collections, tEN, divided by the population of retirees, N, or tE per retiree. That is the same as their past payroll tax payments. With no population growth and no growth of earnings, the rate of return is also zero. Workers get back just what they paid in—no more, no less.

Now assume that each successive cohort has total earnings that are higher than the one before by some amount, say, $100Z$ percent. This growth can arise because either population or earnings per worker increases.

If earnings for the oldest cohort, the group that is currently retired, was EN, and the earnings of the working cohort is $(1 + Z)EN$, the retired cohort paid payroll taxes of tE per person. Its benefits, based on the payroll taxes collected from the next cohort, total $t(1 + Z)EN$. Divided among the N retirees, the benefit per retiree is $t(1 + Z)EN/N = t(1 + Z)E$. Thus the pension is $(1 + Z)$ times larger than the taxes each retiree paid, providing an economic return of Z, the same as the growth of total earnings.

This example is oversimplified in various ways. Work lives are typically longer than retirement. Growth of population and earnings per worker varies from year to year. Payroll tax rates and benefit formulas change over time. Benefits may be more generous for some workers than for others based on earnings or family circumstances. But on the average and over time, the basic proposition holds—the real rate of return under pay-as-you-go social insurance equals the growth of real earnings.

TO ACCUMULATE OR NOT TO ACCUMULATE?

A lot of ink has been spilled in intellectually spirited debates over whether Social Security initially should have been financed on a pay-as-you-go basis, or whether reserves should have been accumulated.

BOX 3–6
WHY VOLUNTARY SOCIAL SECURITY CANNOT WORK

Some commentators on Social Security have urged that workers be permitted to "opt out" of the program as long as they can demonstrate that they are personally saving at least as much as they would have paid in payroll taxes. That approach, its supporters maintain, assures that workers will save, but it does not dictate the form of that saving. Any system that broadens the range of choice, it is argued, must improve individual welfare.

The argument for permitting people to save on their own is appealing—if people want to do something and it isn't illegal, why not let them do it? The answer is that even if people who opt out are correctly making self-interested decisions, their actions reduce the choices of others and are likely to lower overall welfare.

Under pay-as-you-go financing, workers pay taxes now to support current benefit payments of retirees, but claim benefits for themselves later, possibly decades later. Any person who withdraws from the system removes revenues necessary to pay current benefits *to others* and uses those revenues to accumulate reserves *for himself or herself.* If nothing else is done, revenues to sustain current benefits will be insufficient. To sustain these benefits, therefore, some other tax would have to be imposed. Most of the added burden would fall on workers who did not "opt out." Each worker who opts out is able to offload part of his or her share of the costs of supporting current retirees. If, in the end, all workers left the system but benefits for current pensioners were maintained, everyone would face higher taxes because they would collectively need to pay sufficient taxes to sustain benefits as well as make separate deposits to their own accounts.

High earners, single workers, and members of childless families are particularly likely to opt out because Social Security treats them less generously than it does low earners and members of large families. But their withdrawal would threaten the resources needed to sustain the social assistance provided by Social Security because they pay higher taxes relative to promised benefits than does the average worker. By leaving the system and placing their payroll taxes in their own accounts, high earners and members of small families who opt out would escape bearing their share of the cost to achieve these social objectives.

Finally, opting out is not practical because people's circumstances change. Workers marry, have children, get divorced, lose jobs, become disabled, and so on. Savings that seemed adequate under one set of circumstances may prove to be insufficient in other situations. Unless those who opted out had to buy insurance to protect themselves from adverse developments and were required to invest in low-risk assets, some would find themselves dependent on government charity later on. This would impose costs on those workers who did not opt out.

As a practical matter, this debate is pointless. The decisions of the late 1930s and 1940s to pay relatively generous retirement benefits to retirees whose working careers had been blighted by the Great Depression cannot be undone.[11]

NO GAIN WITHOUT PAIN

The question now is whether to build reserves in the future, and if so, how to build them—within the Social Security system or through some alternative defined-contribution pension structure. There is no costless or politically painless way to build reserves. Someone has to pay for them, through either reduced benefits or increased taxes.[12] Cutting benefits would renege, at least in part, on promises to retirees and older workers, imposing hardship on some.

Tax increases can take two forms that are mathematically equivalent but politically very different. Taxes earmarked to Social Security— payroll taxes or a special income tax—can be explicitly increased. Alternatively, general revenues can be transferred to Social Security instead of being used to finance tax cuts.[13] Although the result in both cases is higher taxes, the politics of explicit tax increases and those of a failure to cut taxes (or increase spending) are quite different. In a parallel fashion, the politics of cutting general government spending to pay for transfers to Social Security would be quite different from forgoing spending increases in order to finance such transfers.

If taxes are increased—now or in the future—active workers will not only have to support pensions for current beneficiaries but also to save for their own reserve accumulation. To avoid this choice, some have suggested that all or a portion of the payroll tax should go to build reserves in the personal retirement accounts of young workers and that bonds be issued to pay pensions of retirees and older workers. However, building individual accounts by issuing government bonds would be a financial shell game. Issuing bonds creates no new assets and adds nothing to national saving or productive capacity. The assets in workers' accounts would be exactly matched by new liabilities of the federal government. The real economic benefits come from increased saving, which requires either tax increases or benefit cuts that force workers or beneficiaries to reduce their consumption.

The benefit cuts or tax increases necessary to build reserves are the same whether they help build reserves in Social Security or in individual accounts. Furthermore, the economic effects do not depend on whether Social Security is retained or replaced by private individual accounts (see Box 3–7, page 50). In either case, raising reserves by $1 billion would *directly* boost national saving by the same amount. But the *full* effect on national saving would likely be less than $1 billion, because private account balances might cause individuals to

BOX 3–7
WHAT HAPPENS WHEN WE SAVE $1 BILLION?

PRIVATE SAVING

Private savers save	+ $1 billion
Private saving available for private investment rises	+ $1 billion
U.S.-owned capital stock grows	+ $1 billion

ADDITION TO SOCIAL SECURITY RESERVES

Social security reserves rise	+ $1 billion
Social security trustees buy additional government bonds	+ $1 billion
Government sells fewer bonds to private sector	– $1 billion
Private saving available for private investment rises	+ $1 billion
U.S.-owned capital stock grows	+ $1 billion

*In either case, the return equals $1 billion
multiplied by the private rate of return.*

save less in other forms and increased Social Security reserves might cause elected officials to raise spending or cut taxes elsewhere in the government budget.

ARE THE TRUST FUNDS "REAL"?

Some analysts have claimed that Social Security and Medicare reserves are just accounting mechanisms and that the trust funds hold only "paper" assets. They sometimes claim that the accumulation of large trust fund balances does nothing to improve the government's ability to pay future benefits and that they are available only in "a bookkeeping sense."[14] This view is simply wrong.

This statement confuses two distinct questions: whether trust fund accumulation adds to national saving, investment, and the capacity to pay future pension benefits; and whether government budget operations *on accounts other than Social Security* add to national saving, investment, and the capacity to pay future benefits. Social Security surpluses, which add to trust fund reserves, boost national saving in precisely the same sense that additions to individual retirement accounts add to national saving. Deficits in the *non–Social Security* budget, however, subtract from national saving and can offset the savings-increasing effects of Social Security reserve accumulation.

The first step to sorting out these issues is to recognize that the direct effects on private investment of adding $1 billion to Social Security reserves or to individual accounts are identical, as shown in Box 3–7. Given government spending and revenues *outside* Social Security, a $1 billion cash flow surplus in Social Security and $1 billion of private saving directly add to funds available for private investment in exactly the same way and in the same amount. In each case, the return to the nation is $1 billion multiplied by the marginal productivity of private capital.

Each year from fiscal 1983 through fiscal 1997, Social Security ran surpluses, which added to national saving, but deficits in the rest of the government's operations, which subtracted from national saving, were larger so that, *taken as a whole,* the federal government ran deficits, thereby reducing national saving. In 1998 the Social Security surpluses exceeded the deficit in the rest of the government's operations, and the federal government, overall, added to national savings.

Starting in 1999 the federal government ran surpluses both in Social Security and in the rest of its operations. In no case, however, does the fact that non-Social Security operations of government are in deficit contradict the fact that additions to Social Security reserves add to national savings, unless one believes that lawmakers run deficits in the non-Social Security operations purposefully to offset Social Security surpluses. But the statements of policymakers as well as their actions during the past decade suggest just the opposite: that they wanted to eliminate the deficit in the non-Social Security portion of the budget—and did—even as Social Security surpluses were growing. Therefore, Social Security surpluses add to saving and boost investment, which expands productive capacity, thereby increasing the ability of the federal government and the nation to meet future pension obligations.

The statement that Social Security reserves are only "paper assets" is true at a level that has no significance; it is false in substance. Neither Social Security nor private financial savers, including individuals and pension funds, hold "real" assets in their accounts. Both hold IOUs—paper promises of some private or public entity to pay interest or dividends. In each case, the assets are only as good as the willingness and ability of someone to redeem the assets or buy them before maturity. The only difference between reserves of Social Security and those of private savers is that Social Security's reserves consist entirely of "gilt-edged" federal securities, because U.S. law allows Social Security trustees to invest only in securities guaranteed as to principal and interest by the federal government.

Individual savers, in contrast, are free to invest in private securities, about which the same cannot be said. These assets generally involve some risk because changing market conditions may undermine a company's profitability, its ability to redeem its debt, and the value of its shares. New products or producers may come along that shrink the market for a company's output. The public's taste may shift suddenly to goods other than those the company produces. Or bad management may destroy an otherwise healthy business. To compensate for such risks, private assets must provide higher returns than government bonds. But to consider the stock certificates or bonds of some blue-chip corporation—recall the Penn Central saga—let alone the inflated shares of dot-com or biotech start-ups that have never turned a profit and have few tangible possessions—to be "real" assets and the government securities held in Social Security's reserves not to be "real" is preposterous. Not only does the government have the means to pay its obligations that is unmatched in the private sector, it also has the will, buttressed by political pressures. It is inconceivable that lawmakers would allow the government to renege on its financial promises to redeem bonds held by the trust fund especially when the Social Security surpluses have helped to pay down the national debt, increased national saving and investment, and expanded the nation's productive capacity, making it easier to meet these obligations. Social Security reserves are therefore every bit as real as those held by any private pension fund, personal brokerage account, or corporate reserves.

IS RESERVE ACCUMULATION WORTH THE PAIN?

However reserves are created, the central questions remain: Is the bill worth paying? If so, what is the best way to pay it? The debate on these issues is arcane and technical, and so we present only a few of the arguments that protagonists raise.

The Case against Reserve Accumulation. Opponents of reserve accumulation start by noting that future generations will, almost certainly, be richer than we are. Forcing us to save more reduces our consumption to make our wealthier children and grandchildren richer still. Nothing is stopping us, it is argued, from saving more as individuals if we want to help our heirs. But why should we be forced to do so collectively? Shouldn't this be a matter of individual choice?

Even if more saving is desirable, policies to force saving might not work. If public pensions build reserves and benefits become more secure, people might save less individually or through their company pension plans, or they might borrow more. When the economic dust has settled, total saving may be little changed. It could just take different forms—larger public pension surpluses and less personal net saving. Even if more saving is desirable and saving could be increased by raising pension-related taxes, levies other than the payroll tax may be fairer and more conducive to economic efficiency. Furthermore, if taxes are to be increased, there may be better things to do with those resources than to enrich future generations. Fighting poverty, providing health care to the uninsured, improving educational opportunities, cleaning up the environment, combating crime, and investing in medical research and public infrastructure rank higher than boosting national saving in the judgment of some observers. Many of these activities could improve the lives of both current and future generations.

The Case for Reserve Accumulation. Despite these concerns, we believe that the case for measures to boost national saving is persuasive. Evidence suggests that the lure of current consumption overwhelms prudent planning for future wants so that people consistently save too little for their own good. Furthermore, income taxes and failings of financial markets deny people the full economic returns from saving, and thereby discourage saving. Still others believe that Social Security, Medicare, and other forms of assistance blunt personal incentives to save. Since these programs build reserves smaller than those individuals would have to accumulate to provide themselves equivalent protection, they depress saving.[15]

Finally, many observers doubt that the myriad discrete decisions of individuals and businesses necessarily produce exactly the right amount of saving. They point to two troublesome facts. First, U.S. national saving is lower than it has been in the past—a bit over half as high, measured as a share of total output, as it was during the quarter-century after World War II and lower than the saving of other major industrial nations. Second, the baby boomers are aging. They will soon begin to retire and become dependent on active workers for pensions and health care. Boosting saving, investment, and productivity in anticipation of that event will raise output per worker and relieve future workers of some or all of the burden of supporting the aging baby boomers. So much has been said about the looming costs of the baby boomers—including a great deal that is quite misleading—that we shall devote all of Chapter 4 to this issue.

CONCLUSION

However one comes down on the desirability of boosting saving, the debate about Social Security reform has to face two other core issues. The first concerns how the inescapable risks associated with any pension system should be distributed. This issue shows up as a technical debate over whether the nation's basic mandatory retirement system should be a defined-benefit (DB) pension system or a defined-contribution (DC) pension system. As one wag has put it, "DB or not DB, that is the question." We conclude that the strengths and advantages of a defined-benefit system outweigh those of a defined-contribution system *for the program that is intended to assure basic income during retirement, disability, and survivorship*. Risks in such a program should be broadly shared by society—by high earners and low earners, by big families and small families, by retirees and current and future workers.

The chief argument for imposing these risks on individuals is the claim that individuals will make better saving and investment decisions if they bear these risks themselves than if the risks are diffused more broadly. For most personal financial decisions, the argument for personal responsibility is persuasive. The financial system of the United States depends on risk bearing and provides financial rewards to individuals who bear risk. But the argument that individuals should bear risks carries little weight in the case of the basic pension program. First, individuals are ill-equipped to handle the investment, inflation, longevity, and other risks they would have to shoulder under a defined-contribution pension system.

Second, the prime justification for a mandatory pension system is the recognition that many people will *not* make good decisions about how much to save, how to invest what they have saved, and how rapidly to spend their retirement savings. Many will save too little and end their careers unable to support themselves adequately during retirement or disability. Some will invest too conservatively, in very safe but low-yielding assets that will not grow fast enough to sustain an adequate pension. Some will choose investments that turn out poorly. Most are likely to shun annuities and be exposed to longevity risk. If the experience to date with individual accounts in the United Kingdom is any guide, administrative costs will be high and few will protect their basic pension from inflation by purchasing the inflation-indexed securities now issued by the Treasury Department.[16]

Rather than exposing workers individually to these risks, it would be far better, we believe, to spread them among active and future workers and current beneficiaries. That is precisely what a defined-benefit plan does and what a defined-contribution plan does not do. For these reasons, the defined-benefit character of the Social Security system should be preserved.

A mandatory defined-contribution system could require that contributions be invested in a balanced mix of indexed mutual funds (stocks and bonds, domestic and foreign). Rules could require that all retirees use their accumulated assets to purchase inflation-indexed annuities of at least a minimum value, annuities that covered both workers and their spouses. Nevertheless, such a system would not provide protection from broad swings in asset values that would leave some cohorts much worse off than others.

Nor would it address the second core issue involved in the current debate over the future of the nation's basic pension program, namely, how to provide for the program's social objectives. It is important, we believe, to ensure adequate benefits for low-wage workers and to provide extra benefits for spouses and children of deceased and disabled workers. It is important also to supply some additional support to spouses who have not participated fully in the paid labor force, often because they have devoted much of their time to rearing children or performing unpaid services in schools, churches, hospitals, and other voluntary organizations. Almost all participants in the Social Security reform debate acknowledge the importance of sustaining assistance to support these social functions, as our review of reform plans in Chapter 7 indicates. They do so because they understand that income inequality rose rapidly from 1974 through 1995, that real earnings of unskilled and semiskilled workers actually fell over the same period, and that poverty is a significant problem among the disabled and older surviving spouses of deceased workers. The strong economy of the late 1990s stopped the slide to ever-rising inequality and brought roughly proportional increases in earnings throughout the income distribution. But the need for social protections provided by Social Security remains high. We shall return to this issue when we evaluate the various proposals for Social Security reform.

4

WILL THE BABY BOOMERS
BREAK THE BANK?

Between 2008 and 2026, the 77 million baby boomers born from 1946 through 1964 will become eligible for Social Security. The fraction of the population eligible for retirement benefits—those age 62 and over—will increase from 15.6 percent to 22.6 percent. Unless birth rates rise sharply and unexpectedly or young immigrants flood the country, the elderly will form a permanently larger share of the population. How much will the baby boomers' retirement cost? Will these costs cut into the living standards of active workers if nothing is done to reduce currently promised benefits? What can the nation do now to prepare for these costs during this period of extraordinary prosperity that America is currently enjoying?

THE BURDEN OF SOCIAL SECURITY:
PAST, PRESENT, AND FUTURE

Three measures of the burden of Social Security appear in the popular press and scholarly journals—the ratio of beneficiaries to workers, benefit costs as a percentage of earnings subject to the payroll tax, and benefit costs as a percentage of gross domestic product. All of these measures indicate that the price of paying Social Security benefits will increase, but they differ as to the size of that increase (see Table 4–1).

TABLE 4-1
THREE MEASURES OF THE BURDEN OF SOCIAL SECURITY

Year	Beneficiaries per 100 Workers	Benefit Costs as Percentage of Taxable Payroll	Benefit Costs as Percentage of Gross Domestic Product
2000	29	10.3	4.2
2015	36	12.9	5.0
2030	47	17.4	6.6
2045	49	17.9	6.6
2060	51	18.6	6.7
2075	54	19.5	6.8
Change from 2000 to 2075	+ 86 percent	+ 89 percent	+ 63 percent

Source: 2000 Annual Report of the Board of Trustees of the Federal Old-Age and Survivors Insurance and Disability Insurance Trust Funds, Washington, D.C.: U.S. Government Printing Office, May 30, 2000.

BENEFICIARIES PER WORKER

One of the most widely cited indicators of the economic burden of Social Security is the ratio of beneficiaries to workers.[1] Active workers must produce the food, clothing, shelter, health care, and other goods and services consumed by themselves and their families, by Social Security beneficiaries, and by other members of the population who are not working. In 2000, there were 29 beneficiaries for every 100 covered workers. By 2040, the number will rise to 49, and by 2075 there will be 54 beneficiaries for every 100 workers, suggesting that there will be an 86 percent increase in the burden imposed by Social Security.

Although common, this way of measuring the burden of retirees on the active population is misleading. To understand why, one can consider the case of ordinary pensions. Suppose that workers' premiums, together with earnings on their pension funds, fully paid for the pensions they will receive. Because workers had paid in full for their pensions, most people would agree that these benefits would not burden others, any more than the purchase of a car by one family imposes burdens on others. In each case, the worker-retirees receive something with the same value as the price they paid for it. The practical question, therefore, is whether the payroll taxes of Social Security beneficiaries and their employers are sufficient to purchase the benefits they will receive.

For people reaching age 65 before about 2000, the answer is clearly "no." These workers paid low payroll taxes during much of their working lives; the maximum tax payment in 2000 was more than eight times that of 1958, adjusted for inflation. In the early years of Social Security, low payroll tax rates easily covered the cost of benefits for the few eligible retirees. Most of the elderly at that time were not eligible for benefits because they had stopped working before the system began or had been employed in the 45 percent of jobs not initially covered by Social Security. In 1945, five years after benefits were first paid, only four of every 100 people age 65 and older received benefits and there were only two elderly beneficiaries per 100 workers. By 1950, when only 16 percent of those age 65 and older received benefits, there were six beneficiaries per 100 workers. Not until 1958, when there were seventeen beneficiaries for every 100 workers, were more than half of the elderly receiving Social Security benefits.

In contrast, the payroll taxes paid by cohorts of workers born after about 1935 and their employers are sufficient to purchase the retirement, survivor's, and disability benefits they are going to receive. In this sense, the baby boomers are not generating any new burdens on the active workers even though they are more numerous than their predecessors.

If the retirement of the baby boomers is not responsible for the projected long-term deficit in Social Security, what is? The answer lies in the fact that *previous* generations of workers received much larger benefits than were warranted by the payroll taxes they and their employers had paid. Much of the extra benefits, approved by successive Congresses and administrations, went to generations part of whose working careers predated Social Security and had been marred by the Great Depression. During the 1940s, 1950s, and 1960s these extra benefits kept many elderly off of Old Age Assistance—the welfare program for the aged of that era. As a result, a substantial portion of the payroll taxes paid by the baby boomers and their older brothers and sisters went to pay the benefits of their parents, grandparents, and great-grandparents rather than accumulating to support their own pensions.

Whatever the merits of those transfers, they cannot be undone. They produced what is loosely known as the "unfunded liability"— the gap between benefit obligations to future retirees and the reserves accumulated on their behalf. The unfunded liability was estimated to be about $3 trillion in 2000, assuming that workers continue to pay taxes and to claim benefits as specified under current law. If generous benefits had not been paid in the early years of Social Security, the unfunded liability would not have accumulated and reserves, together with projected tax collections, would be more than sufficient to cover all benefits promised the baby boomers under current law, despite the drop in the ratio of workers to Social Security beneficiaries. It is the unfunded liability, rather than pensions for baby boomers, that accounts for the projected long-term deficit in Social Security.

BENEFIT COSTS, TAXABLE EARNINGS, AND GDP

The payroll taxes levied on future workers and the share of GDP devoted to benefits also are projected to rise. Under current law, Social Security benefits as a share of taxable earnings are projected to increase over the next seventy-five years from 10.3 percent to 19.5 percent, a rise of 89 percent. Outgo as a share of GDP is projected to rise from 4.2 percent to 6.8 percent, a rise of 63 percent. The difference between these two growth rates is largely attributable to the assumption that workers will receive an increasing fraction of their total compensation in the form of untaxed "fringe" benefits, such as health insurance.

These cost ratios can be reduced in only two ways: by cutting benefits or raising the growth of taxable earnings and GDP. However, even if the cost ratios are unchanged, the nation can decide *when* to pay the taxes to support these benefits and *who* should pay them. It can pay the taxes as the costs come due—pay-as-you-go financing. In that event, taxes will rise gradually in line with benefit costs. Alternatively, taxes can be raised before costs rise, building up financial reserves. These financial reserves would have a physical counterpart—namely, increased investment that added to productive capacity. The income from these investments, and possibly the principal as well, could then be used to reduce the taxes that future workers would otherwise have to pay. Similarly, the nation can decide whether to collect these taxes, now or later, from workers in proportion to their earnings—that is, through the payroll tax. Or it can collect these taxes from general taxpayers in proportion to their incomes—that is, from personal and corporate income taxes.

Just how much will the burden of supporting the elderly and disabled grow as the baby boomers retire? Between 2000 and 2045 Social Security spending as a share of GDP is projected to rise 2.4 percentage points. This increase slightly exceeds the 2 percent of GDP growth in the cost of Social Security that took place in the twelve years between 1970 and 1982, a period less than a third as long. It is roughly one-third of the growth of defense spending as a share of GDP—7.3 percentage points—that occurred between 1948 and 1955 when the cold war intensified. It is slightly more than the 2.1 percentage points of GDP increase in federal spending on Medicare and Medicaid between 1980 and 1997. These increases were large but did not cause political crises or significant economic dislocation.

But Social Security is far from the whole story when it comes to the burden that retirement of baby boomers will impose on society. Between 2000 and 2045, Medicare spending is projected to increase by 2.5 percentage points of GDP. Medicaid spending, roughly two-thirds of which provides health services to low-income elderly and disabled persons, is projected to increase by about 2.4 percentage points of GDP over the same period. In addition, the budgetary costs of Supplementary Security Income (SSI) and food stamp benefits for the low-income aged and disabled and private expenditures on long-term care are likely to grow as well.

The projected increase in the cost of Social Security alone, or in combination with Medicare and the other programs, is significant but is not likely to overwhelm future economic growth. If real per capita income grows 1.2 percent annually—considerably slower than the 2 percent at which per capita output rose from 1990 through 1999—real GDP per person will rise 61 percent by 2040.[2] Of this amount, slightly less than one-third would be needed to deal with the projected increase in the cost of Social Security and Medicare assuming *nothing* is done to curb the growth of spending on these programs. Thus, moderate economic growth would enable future workers both to enjoy rising living standards and to pay the added taxes necessary to sustain currently projected benefit costs. Reserve accumulation in both programs that translates into increased national investment and economic growth would alleviate this pressure.

The decision to levy higher taxes would, however, still be difficult and divisive.

BENEFICIARIES AND WORKERS

As should be apparent, the emphasis on the declining ratio of workers to beneficiaries is misleading. But even if one focuses on this misleading indicator, two facts should not be ignored.

First, workers support not only the elderly but also children and nonaged adults. While the proportion of the population that is elderly has risen and will increase further, the proportion of children and nonaged adults who are not working for pay has fallen over the past three decades and is projected to fall further in the future. Consequently, the number of people each worker will support is projected to rise only modestly—approximately 6 percent—between now and 2040, even though the number of elderly will soar (see Figure 4–1). The number of economically inactive members of the population per 100 workers was much higher in the past (156 in 1960) than it was in the mid-1990s (103 in 1995) or than it is projected to be in the future (115 in 2040).

Second, not all members of the inactive population generate equal costs, and those costs appear in different budgets. The average aged or disabled person costs more to support than the average child. Children and their nonworking caretakers typically live in multiperson families that enjoy economies of scale in living expenses. The elderly and disabled typically live alone or in two-person households. Children generate costs for publicly supported education but consume only about one-third as much health care on the average as does an elderly person.[3] But, on balance, an aging population means that the costs of supporting the inactive population shift from private to public budgets.

BUDGET PROSPECTS

During the late 1990s, federal budgetary prospects improved dramatically. The accumulation of reserves in Social Security accelerated. In 1997, projections indicated that reserves in 2025 would be $1.9 trillion; by 2000, the projected balance for 2025 had more than tripled to $6 trillion. Projections still indicate that benefit costs will eventually

FIGURE 4-1
MOUTHS TO FEED
POPULATION PER WORKER, 1950–2042

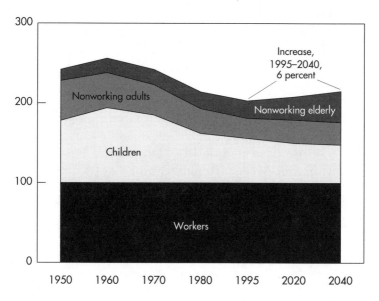

Source: National Academy of Social Insurance, "How Many People Does Each Worker Support?" *Social Insurance Update* 2, no. 4 (April 1997).

deplete these reserves and that a long-run deficit remains. The strong economy, which has improved the financial prospects of Social Security, has even more strikingly brightened the fiscal horizons in the rest of the federal budget. In 1999, the rest of the budget moved into surplus, ending an unbroken string of deficits dating back to 1960. Current projections indicate that if lawmakers leave the tax code and entitlement programs unchanged, and if they allow other spending to increase with inflation, the surpluses in the non-Social Security portion of the budget will grow steadily. Even under more realistic assumptions that include modest tax cuts and slightly faster growth in spending, this part of the budget is likely to remain in surplus in the foreseeable future.

The dramatic improvement in budget prospects has raised again the option of using general revenues to support Social Security. This method of finance was widely discussed during the debates surrounding enactment of the Social Security Act. Indeed, some proponents of old-age pensions felt so strongly about the desirability of partial general revenue financing that they opposed the Social Security Act because Congress, at the urging of President Roosevelt, decided to rely exclusively on the payroll tax.

Several proposals have emerged that would use these projected surpluses to help close the projected long-term Social Security deficit. Some would transfer general revenues directly to Social Security, thereby filling in part of the unfunded liability. President Clinton, for example, proposed *direct* general revenue transfers to the Social Security trust fund starting in 2011. Vice President Gore endorsed this policy during his presidential campaign. Others would use general revenues *indirectly* to close projected deficits. During the 106th Congress, Representatives Bill Archer (Republican of Texas) and Clay Shaw (Republican of Florida), for example, endorsed the use of general revenues to help fund private accounts that would be converted into pensions, most of which would be offset by cuts in Social Security benefits. The improved budgetary climate means that general revenues are likely to figure prominently in any Social Security reform legislation. We shall describe these issues more fully in Chapters 6 and 7.

What Can We Do About It?

Americans can act now to lighten the future burden of supporting the baby boomers in three ways. Congress can cut future benefits. It can raise the rate of return on Social Security's reserves. Or it can adopt policies to increase economic growth. In Chapter 6 we present a menu of measures to restore balance to Social Security that includes benefit reductions and a proposal to increase the return on the trust fund's reserves. Here we review two ways to boost economic growth—expanding the total number of workers and making each worker more productive.

Enlarging the Workforce

Faster population growth eventually enlarges the labor force and the economy's productive capacity. Unfortunately, few effective and politically acceptable ways exist to raise population growth. Current fertility rates would just about sustain an unchanged population if there were no net immigration. Fertility rates are not projected to increase, and there is little evidence that acceptable public policy initiatives can do much to raise them. Furthermore, even if birthrates could be increased, it would take decades before the additional children were educated, reached adulthood, entered the labor force in significant numbers, and affected national production. Increased immigration can boost the labor force rapidly. But Social Security projections now assume a net immigration rate of 900,000 a year, and current rates of immigration are already producing economic and social strains.

Within the limits set by the adult population, the labor force can grow only if an increased proportion of adults choose to work for pay. The scope for such increase is limited, however, because the proportion of adults working for pay is already at a historic high. Sixty percent of women now work for pay outside the home, up from 38 percent in 1960, and Social Security's long-run projections already assume that an even higher fraction of women will enter the paid labor force in the future. Large additional increases are unlikely.

The story for nonaged men is rather different. As women have moved into the paid labor force, men—especially those age 50 to 65—have moved out, largely through earlier retirement. The proportion of 65-year-old men in the paid labor force has dropped from 67 percent in 1940 to 35 percent in 1998–99 (Figure 4–2, page 66). This trend reflects the fundamental economic fact that as people grow richer they want to have more leisure, which they get through shorter work weeks, longer vacations, and earlier retirement.

Social Security and private pensions have made earlier retirement possible for workers who have little personal savings. In fact, private pensions in the past expressly encouraged retirement of older and more highly compensated workers. To achieve this result, pensions for workers rose little or not at all after they reached a certain age. Social Security, in contrast, is roughly neutral with respect to retirement for workers up to age 65 because pensions for those who continue to work past age 61 are increased approximately enough to compensate for the forgone pensions.[4]

After dropping for decades, labor force participation rates of older males have inched up since the late 1980s. It is unclear whether the trend toward ever-earlier retirement has stopped permanently or has merely paused in response to an unusually strong economy, as

FIGURE 4–2

MALE LABOR FORCE PARTICIPATION RATES, 1910–99

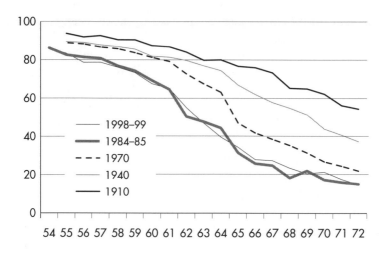

Sources: Data from 1910 are from Roger L. Ransom, Richard Sutch, and Samuel H. Williamson, "Retirement Past and Present," in Alicia H. Munnell, ed., *Retirement and Public Policy* (Dubuque, Iowa: Kendall/Hunt, 1991), p. 45; data from 1940 and 1970 are from Alicia Munnell, *The Future of Social Security* (Washington, D.C.: Brookings Institution Press, 1977), p. 70; data from 1984–85 and 1998–99 are from Gary Burtless tabulations of March CPS data from 1984, 1985, 1998, and 1999.

happened during the boom years of the 1960s. Policy changes have made it easier for older workers to remain in the labor force. Bans on discrimination against older workers were enacted in 1967 and 1990. Employer-imposed mandatory retirement rules were prohibited in 1986. Businesses are now required to continue pension contributions on behalf of those who work past the normal retirement age. In addition, the increment in Social Security benefits for those who work past age 65 was raised. Some analysts think that the trend toward ever earlier retirements has been reversed, while others believe that the long-term trend is likely soon to reassert itself.[5] We will not know for several years whether men have decided to work longer or are just adjusting to a new policy environment and taking advantage of the strong economy.

If older workers could be encouraged to work even a bit longer, the effect on the labor force could be significant. For example, if men age

55 and older could be encouraged to work at the same rates as they did in 1970, the labor force would be enlarged by 2.9 million, which is one-fifth of the total projected labor force growth over the next decade.

The most obvious ways to encourage later retirement involve changing Social Security and Medicare. Social Security benefits could be cut either across the board, or just for early retirees, to encourage older workers to remain in the labor force. The age of initial entitlement could be raised. The delayed retirement credit—the increase in future benefits provided to compensate those whose benefits are cut because of the earnings test—could be further increased. In 2000, Congress repealed, for those 65 and older, the retirement test—the reduction in benefits that was imposed when earnings exceeded specified thresholds. Changes in Medicare rules could reduce costs to employers of retaining workers past age 65. Medicare currently pays benefits to such workers only to the extent that private, employer-sponsored insurance plans do not cover costs. If Medicare were the primary payer, the health care costs to businesses for older workers would be reduced.

Raising the Age at which "Full" Benefits Are Paid. The age at which unreduced retirement benefits are paid—the so-called normal retirement age—is 65 for all workers born before 1938. In 1983, Congress approved legislation that will increase this age to 67 over the 2000 to 2022 period.[6] Many people refer to this change as an "increase in the retirement age." That designation is inaccurate. The change in law does not increase the age of initial entitlement, and it lowers benefits proportionally for all ages. Deeper benefit cuts brought about by further increases in the age at which unreduced benefits are paid might cause some older workers to defer retirement, although empirical estimates indicate that the effects would be small.

Early Retirement Benefits. The availability of Social Security benefits at age 62 facilitates early retirement, even if it does not penalize continued work. More men retire at age 62 than at any other age—15 percent of those still working. However, claiming benefits before the "full-benefits" age permanently lowers benefits not only for the worker but also for the surviving spouse. A larger early-retirement penalty might cause some people to continue working. Unfortunately, it could also increase poverty among survivors of workers who retired early anyway. Already, 21 percent of women age 65 and older who live alone are poor, and a little less than half have incomes below 150 percent of the poverty threshold.

Age of Initial Entitlement. Neither of the two previous benefit cuts would alter the age at which benefits are first available. Although life expectancy at age 62 has increased by 3.3 years since 1961, when men first became eligible for early retirement benefits, raising the age of initial entitlement has not been politically popular. While far less true today than in decades past, some workers develop physical and mental limitations or are employed in strenuous jobs that make work past age 61 increasingly onerous. In addition, raising the age of initial entitlement saves little money in the long run because the increase in benefits associated with delaying retirement from age 62 to age 65 approximately offsets the shorter period over which benefits must be paid. Raising the age of initial entitlement from 62 to 63 or 64 might well encourage continued work, however. Unlike the two previous benefit cuts, it would not risk permanently lowering benefits for surviving spouses.

The Delayed Retirement Credit. In addition to raising the age at which unreduced benefits are paid, Congress in 1983 also liberalized the "delayed retirement credit"—the increase in benefits paid to those who work past the age at which unreduced benefits are paid and to those who earn enough to have their benefits reduced by the earnings test. When this change is fully phased in for those reaching age 62 in 2005, the increase will approximately compensate an average worker for the value of benefits lost because of the retirement test. In other words, the lifetime value of benefits the average worker can expect to receive will be independent of when that worker chooses to retire. Raising the delayed retirement credit still more—in effect, subsidizing later retirement—could further encourage work by the elderly but not without increasing program costs.

The Retirement Test. Social Security was conceived as a program to replace lost earnings. Consequently, it has traditionally paid benefits only when the earnings of those age 62 and older were below specified thresholds. This "retirement test" was remarkably unpopular. Many members of Congress long regarded the restriction as unfair and thought that it discouraged work by older men and women. Consequently, Congress steadily raised the amounts people could earn without loss of benefits and abolished it effective in 1983 for workers age 70 or older. In 2000, Congress repealed the test for workers who have reached the full-benefits age. The retirement test still applies to workers who claim benefits before the full-benefits age. Their benefits will be reduced $1 for every $2 of earnings above $10,680 in 2001; this amount will be indexed for inflation in later years.[7]

Strictly economic considerations suggest that the repeal of the retirement test for people above the full-benefits age will not much affect work effort. To begin with, the delayed retirement credit is close to being actuarially equivalent to repeal of the retirement test and will be fully equivalent in 2005. As a result, repeal of the retirement test brings no net economic benefit to average retirees if they have enough savings to balance annual income and spending needs. Furthermore, only about one-third of workers are still in the labor force when they reach the full-benefits age, and fewer than half of them earn more than the $30,000 at which the retirement test would have applied starting in 2002. In other words, workers with average life expectancies will receive the same total lifetime benefits whether they retire at age 62 or continue working and have their benefits reduced because their earnings exceed the retirement test thresholds. However, workers may respond less to a fair delayed retirement credit than they would to higher thresholds or a repeal of the earnings test, which would let more retirees receive pensions while continuing to work.[8]

Relaxation or repeal of the retirement test may have unintended side effects. In particular, it may strengthen arguments for income testing of benefits, as Social Security pensions would be paid to some people who were also taking home very high salaries, contrary to the traditional goal of the system—to "replace lost earnings."[9] Furthermore, repealing the earnings test boosts government spending in the short run.

While repeal of the retirement test and possible increases in the delayed retirement credit are unlikely to increase work by older workers much, delaying the availability of retirement benefits beyond age 62 would discourage retirement of people who lack the liquid assets to do so. This change in benefit structure is the one most likely to boost the labor supply of older Americans. The burden of such a change would fall most heavily on groups with relatively short life expectancies, including blacks, Native Americans, and low-earners in general.

BOOSTING THE GROWTH OF OUTPUT PER WORKER

Increasing output per worker will lighten the burden of supporting a growing aged population. How fast output per worker grows depends on changes in the skills of workers, on the quantity and quality of capital that workers use, and on managerial skills and business organization.

Skills. Improved education and on-the-job training increase worker productivity and earnings. They are desirable for reasons that have nothing to do with Social Security. But they also can help the nation meet pension costs by raising payroll tax collections. Neither individuals nor businesses normally take this connection into account when deciding how much education or training is optimal. As important as education and training may be to economic growth, public policy in this area will continue to be driven more by the desire to expand individual opportunity than by any notion that a more skilled workforce could ease the societal burden of supporting an expanding population of retirees. Nevertheless, measures to improve the quality of education and to increase the number of young people graduating from high schools, colleges, and training programs do help ease pension costs. The benefits are very slow in coming, however, because most of the labor force for the next several decades will have completed its formal education before any improvement could occur.

Technology, Management, and Capital. Technological advances, investment, improved management, and better business organization all boost economic growth. Public policy can promote technological advances by supporting basic and applied research and by education. Competitive and open markets, judicious and limited regulation, and a tax system that distorts investment decisions as little as possible also facilitate managerial and technological innovation, which, in turn, favor rapid economic advance.

How the nation's basic pension system is financed affects national saving, which, along with net investment by foreigners, determines the growth of the nation's capital stock. Private saving by U.S. households and businesses declined sharply from an average of more than 10 percent of net national product (NNP) during the period 1960 through 1989 and reached a low of 4.7 percent of NNP in 1999. The drop in household saving was even more striking, from an average of more than 7 percent of NNP in the 1960-89 period to 1.8 percent of NNP in 1999 and less than zero in 2000. This trend is startling, as retirement saving was expected to rise in the late 1980s and 1990s when the baby boomers moved into their prime earning years and their children began to leave home. Reduced tax rates and new tax-sheltered savings accounts should have amplified this trend. The fact that private saving fell is both puzzling and troubling.

The recent history of government saving is quite different and more heartening. Before the mid-1970s, combined revenues of federal, state, and local governments exceeded their spending, which meant the government sector added to national saving. For two decades starting in the mid-1970s, mushrooming federal deficits swamped the small surpluses of states and localities. The government sector as a whole became a net borrower, absorbing private saving that otherwise would have been available for investment. However, the unified federal budget has moved from a deficit of 4.7 percent of GDP in 1992 to a surplus of 2.4 percent of GDP in 2000, thereby raising national saving by about 7 percent of GDP. Official budget projections in mid-2000 suggested that the federal surpluses will gradually rise to more than 4 percent of GDP by 2010, should Congress and the president resist the temptation to use the surpluses to cut taxes and boost spending. Under that assumption, overall budget surpluses should continue indefinitely, even after Social Security and Medicare rise to meet the demands of aging baby boomers.

But budget surpluses are hard to sustain because the benefits of fiscal frugality are deferred and widely diffused. In particular, George W. Bush promised large tax cuts duing his successful presidential campaign. Nevertheless, preserving the surpluses is the most reliable way to boost economic growth and help offset the added costs of supporting the baby boomers in retirement.

CONCLUSION: POLITICS VERSUS ECONOMICS

One can hardly turn on a television or open a newspaper or magazine without encountering overwrought rhetoric bewailing the insupportable burden that the baby boomers will impose on thinned ranks of future workers. From an economic standpoint, this rhetoric is detached from reality. It is not the rise in the fraction of the population that is old that accounts for the projected long-term deficit in Social Security. Rather, it is the fact that modern America has inherited the consequences of decisions of successive Congresses and presidents to pay benefits to retirees early in the life of the Social Security program well beyond the value of the payroll taxes those retirees and their former employers had paid. The challenge America faces today is to decide whether to place the burden for covering this unfunded liability on future workers through the Social Security system or to treat this cost as a general societal responsibility that should be paid for out of general revenues.

The political problems of meeting the costs of population aging are substantial, however. Whether the United States of 2050 and 2075 is merely a bit richer or much richer than it is today, it will still be necessary to shift more of what the economy produces from workers to the elderly and disabled and to survivors of deceased workers. These transfers will require increased taxes if currently promised benefits remain unchanged. Under the current structure, that means higher earmarked payroll taxes. The simplest way to reduce such payroll tax increases is to rely on higher general revenues, transfering general revenues to Social Security. Current or additional tax revenues would go farther to meet benefit promises if Social Security's reserves were invested in assets that generate higher yields than the current portfolio of Treasury securities. Replacing Social Security with mandatory private saving in personal accounts that were invested in private assets is an alternative approach to increasing the yield on reserves; this approach, however, in no way would reduce the burden imposed by Social Security's unfunded liability. We shall examine in Chapter 5 various proposals to make this shift to the private sector and in Chapter 6 how to restore balance in Social Security.

5

PRIVATIZATION

As the twentieth century comes to a close, private enterprises oper-ating in competitive markets stand triumphant around the world. Free markets have proven themselves the most efficient way to produce and distribute most goods and services. In virtually all countries, state-run monopolies and nationalized industries have been marked by in-efficiency, high costs, shoddy quality, and a lack of innovation. Against this backdrop, almost any call to convert to private management a government activity that the private sector has successfully performed merits a serious and sympathetic hearing. Because many elements of Social Security, such as pension management and insurance, resemble services that the private sector delivers successfully, the strengths and weaknesses of privatizing Social Security are well worth examining.

The requirement that people save is one of Social Security's strengths. Other than a few extreme libertarians—who believe that gov-ernment should make no laws restricting individual behavior and should impose no taxes other than those necessary to provide for national defense and ensure public safety—almost no one favors making saving for old-age, retirement, and disability pensions voluntary. Virtually everyone understands that without requirements or powerful incentives, many people would save too little for retirement and carry too little dis-ability and life insurance. Accordingly, virtually all who favor privati-zation of Social Security—"privatizers" for short—acknowledge the need to compel or encourage people to save for old age and protect against the risks that they or a principal earner will become disabled or die, leaving their families with inadequate means of support.

What Is Privatization?

Privatizing Social Security entails two fundamental steps: first, establishing a defined-contribution pension system with individually owned personal retirement accounts, and second, gradually scaling back or eliminating current Social Security retirement benefits. Contributions to personal retirement accounts, like Social Security payroll taxes, would be mandatory. Instead of supporting defined-benefit pensions for current and future workers, these payments would be deposited in individually owned, defined-contribution accounts. The funds in these accounts would be managed by private financial institutions selected by either individuals or the government. The total balances in these accounts—the contributions plus the investment returns—would be available to support a pension for the account's owner.

The balance in each worker's account would depend on how much was contributed, the account's investment returns, and administrative costs. Workers could end up with different balances when they retired, even if they made identical contributions throughout their working years, because they invested in different assets or were charged different administrative fees. Similarly, workers who invested in the same assets managed by the same financial institution could end up with different pensions if some retired when asset prices were high and others when asset prices were low.

Privatization plans differ in several key respects: how much of Social Security the personal accounts would replace; what rules would govern investments; how benefits would be distributed; and how the transition to the new system would be handled.

Scope and Distribution

Some privatization plans would scale back Social Security and supplement these reduced benefits with pensions financed from mandatory saving in personal retirement accounts. Other plans would replace the entire old-age insurance benefit with a new defined-contribution system. Almost all privatization plans would retain the disability and survivor's insurance programs, but cut these benefits. These two programs account for about 30 percent of the total cost of Social Security.

Because balances in defined-contribution accounts accumulate slowly, only about 25 percent of the pension a worker will accumulate over a forty-year career will have accrued after twenty years.[1] As a result, the balances in individual accounts would usually be insufficient to provide adequate survivor's or disability benefits for workers who died or became disabled in their 30s, 40s, or even 50s. Privatization plans could require that workers buy private life and disability insurance policies of a certain minimum size. If the social assistance functions of Social Security were to be sustained, however, many low earners and large families would need supplementary assistance to afford such insurance. In the end, private disability and survivor's programs that contained regulations to prevent insurers from discriminating against workers with high risks would probably resemble current government programs. But they would be more costly to administer—because of sales expenses, loss of economies of scale in record-keeping, and added costs of managing reserves.

Most, but not all, privatization plans would provide larger retirement benefits in relation to earnings and contributions to low earners than to high earners. Some would do this by retaining a scaled-back Social Security program. Others would create a new flat benefit to accompany the defined-contribution pension system. And some would have the government supplement the contributions of low earners to the defined-contribution plan.

INVESTMENT RULES

The first-generation privatization plans proposed that investments be individually managed. Workers would be permitted to invest their retirement accounts in any approved financial asset, much as owners of existing Individual Retirement Accounts (IRAs) now can do. Careful study has indicated that the administrative costs of such plans would be prohibitive. Most accounts would contain small balances, and many administrative costs are more or less the same for large and small accounts.[2] In addition, if individuals managed their accounts, some would invest foolishly and end up with few or no assets for retirement. In response to such considerations, many recent privatization proposals require that investments be managed through government-certified private financial organizations or by the government itself. In either case, account holders would be limited to investments in a few publicly managed stock, bond, or money market index funds, similar to those currently available to federal employees under the Thrift Savings Plan (TSP). Restrictions such as these curtail individual control over accounts but reduce administrative costs. Such limitations also reduce the likelihood that the returns of some participants fall far short of broad market rates of return.

POST-RETIREMENT REGULATION

Under some plans individuals could do what they want with their account balances once they retire—withdraw funds gradually or all at once, buy an annuity, or hold their funds for their heirs. To prevent retirees from squandering their savings, becoming impoverished, and ending up on welfare, other plans would require retirees to make phased withdrawals over a number of years or buy an annuity with all or part of the retirement account balances. Some would require that the annuity purchased by married retirees be a joint annuity.

TRANSITION

The transition from Social Security to a privatized system would pose knotty financial problems. Because reserves were not accumulated for current retirees, active workers' payroll taxes mostly cover the costs of pensions for *previous* generations of workers who are now retired, and only a minor fraction of current taxes goes to building up pension reserves. In 2000, approximately 75 percent of the income flowing into the Social Security system—tax revenues and interest earnings on the reserves—supported pensions for *previous* generations of workers who are now retired.

Under a privatized system, workers would contribute to their own personal retirement accounts. However, unless contribution rates were increased sharply, it would take close to a full working life to build a fund sufficient, on the average, to provide an adequate pension. Consequently, a new defined-contribution system could fully replace current Social Security benefits only for younger workers—say, those under about age 35. Since current retirees and workers over the age of 50 or 55 would have little or no accumulation in private accounts, most privatization plans continue to rely entirely on the current Social Security system for these age groups. Workers of intermediate age would receive benefits partly under the new system and partly under the old.

Paying for Private Accounts. If all or a portion of the contributions of current workers went into personal retirement accounts, extra revenues would be needed to pay for the benefits of current retirees and those older workers still under the current system. Some privatization plans permanently or temporarily raise payroll taxes. One plan would redirect payroll taxes to individual accounts and pay for Social Security benefits with a new 10 percent national sales tax that would gradually phase out as the benefit promises for current retirees and older workers were fulfilled.

Because new taxes are never popular, supporters of privatization have developed ways to soften the blow. One such solution is to spread the costs of the transition over many years by raising taxes only a bit. The revenue generated by this new tax would not cover the initial costs of benefits for workers retired under the old system, and the government would have to borrow to meet the shortfall. Eventually, the revenue from the new tax would be more than enough to pay benefits to retirees still under the old or hybrid systems because death would reduce the ranks of the former while the latter would need smaller and smaller amounts to supplement their growing individual accounts. The excess would be used to retire the debt issued during the early years of the transition. While borrowing reduces the additional taxes that have to be paid in the early years, higher taxes must be imposed for more years to cover interest on the early loans and eventually to pay them off.

General Revenues. Since 1998, when projections began to indicate that the non-Social Security budget would be in surplus, some advocates of privatization have turned to general revenue transfers, rather than payroll tax increases, to pay for transition costs. If the surpluses were large enough to finance transfers to individual accounts, this use of the surpluses, like paying down the public debt, would boost national saving because the alternative uses of surpluses, tax cuts or government spending increases, would boost private consumption (tax cuts) or public consumption (spending increases). Transferring these surpluses to the Social Security trust fund also would boost national saving.

If the government borrowed to finance such transfers because non–Social Security budget surpluses were insufficient to finance general revenue transfers to individual accounts, then such transfers would not raise national saving. Each dollar deposited in individual accounts—an addition to private saving—would be exactly offset by one dollar of borrowing by the federal government—a subtraction from public saving. Since national saving is the sum of private and public saving, the two transactions would cancel out.

However it is handled, the transition to a privatized system will be costly and lengthy. If all payroll taxes were immediately diverted to individual accounts, the total transition cost would be approximately $11 trillion. This amount is the excess over current Social Security reserves that would be required to fund fully the new defined-contribution accounts and to pay all benefits accrued under the Social Security system to current workers and retirees before the creation of the new system.[3] Because this sum is very large, designers of privatization plans keep annual costs manageable by spreading them over time. As a result, the cumulative transition costs for total replacement of Social Security by individual accounts would greatly exceed $11 trillion, much as payments to amortize a home mortgage sum to much more than the amount borrowed. The larger the annual transition cost payments, however, the shorter their duration. Typically, transition costs continue for four or five decades, and in some plans the transition payments continue indefinitely—as is the case with mortgages that require payment only of interest.

A decision to privatize Social Security would mean that, for several decades, workers or the general taxpayer would have to pay not only to build up personal account balances, but also to support pensions for older workers and retirees who were not part of the new system. This consequence is unavoidable because Social Security has an "unfunded liability"—the excess of benefit obligations to retirees and current workers over accumulated reserves. It will be necessary to pay this unfunded liability whether Social Security is privatized or the current system is retained, as we recommend in Chapter 6.[4]

ADVANTAGES OF PRIVATIZATION

Advocates of privatization claim benefits both for individuals and for society. Since plans differ, so do the advantages claimed for them. We gloss over some of the differences to facilitate consideration of the advantages of the privatization approach in general. But it is important to keep in mind that some forms of privatization are demonstrably superior to others.[5]

INCREASED RETIREMENT INCOMES

The primary attraction of privatization to individuals is the claim that it would significantly increase retirement incomes. Privatizers point out that annual real returns on investments in common stocks have averaged 8.3 percent over the past forty years and 13.6 percent over the past twenty years, far in excess of the projected returns on Social Security over the next thirty-five years of only about 1 percent.[6]

These comparisons are misleading for three reasons. First, most Social Security contributions are devoted to paying benefits to current retirees rather than to building investable balances. Workers, or taxpayers more generally, would have to meet these obligations under a privatized system just as they now must do. These payments generate a return of –100 percent, dragging down the overall yield. Unless a privatization plan were to renege on current benefit commitments, it would have to continue to make these same payments. The –100 percent return on this part of the private plan would drag down its rate of return exactly as it does that on Social Security.

Second, the higher yield on additional funds invested in individual accounts has nothing to do with *privatization*. Rather, it arises from the requirement that Social Security reserves be invested in relatively low-yielding government securities, while individual accounts are assumed to be invested in some mix of private stocks and bonds. If Social Security reserves were invested in assets similar to those used to estimate the returns on personal retirement accounts, the average returns of Social Security and a privatized system would be similar. Third, one should include differences in administrative costs, which we examine later in this chapter.

INDIVIDUAL CONTROL AND SELF-RELIANCE

Most people like to have a hand in making important decisions that personally affect them. This preference reflects the American emphasis on self-reliance, individual freedom, and responsibility. Privatization clearly would represent a move to empower individuals.

From its earliest days, critics worried that Social Security would undermine self-reliance by protecting people from the full consequences of their own imprudence. Others simply deplored government interference in an activity—saving and insuring to provide protection against income loss—that they believed individuals could and should perform for themselves. Few now argue that Social Security has caused moral decay, but many believe that it has reduced personal saving.

Supporters of privatization claim that people should exercise increased control over and responsibility for their well-being during retirement. Millions already manage investments made through their company-sponsored, defined-contribution retirement plans. Everyone has considerable discretion about how to invest voluntary savings. Supporters of privatization think it is now appropriate for individuals to exercise more control over the investment of the mandatory saving that is the foundation of their retirement income.

Even though individuals should control their own lives as much as possible, most agree that some limits are necessary. The gains from individual control must be weighed against other goals, such as keeping administrative costs reasonable and ensuring pension adequacy. Administrative costs and the variability of returns rise when people invest in diverse assets. Because record keeping and mailings cost the same for large and small accounts, overhead costs are proportionately larger when the average account is small than when it is large. Costs are minimized if account administration is centralized in a single entity. They are somewhat higher if participants can choose among a few financial institutions. They are much higher if many fund managers advertise to attract clients and workers can shift their accounts from manager to manager. In brief, limiting workers to a few indexed funds holds down administrative costs, which increase steadily as investment choice is broadened. The annual costs of a completely decentralized system like that of current IRAs might exceed those of a centralized system like Social Security by as much as 1 to 2 percent of funds held on deposit. Such an annual difference lowers lifetime accumulations 20 to 40 percent.[7]

Allowing individuals wide latitude over the investment of their mandatory retirement savings has risks as well as benefits. Even the sophisticated sometimes fall prey to scams or exercise bad judgment. But most Americans have little experience managing investment funds. Less than half of the U.S. population has a tax-sheltered, individually managed retirement account. Only one-fifth directly own mutual fund shares or common stocks. Fewer than one in five has accumulated liquid assets equal to the income they earn in one year.[8]

These facts do not mean that private accounts are a bad idea—the long-run growth of U.S. financial markets testifies to their potential. Rather, administrative costs and the limited investment experience of the average worker suggest that relying exclusively on loosely regulated personal retirement accounts is risky. Some investors would take excessive risks in the search for high returns. Others would be excessively cautious, choosing low-yielding assets that would produce inadequate retirement benefits. Unless sales practices of financial institutions authorized to manage personal retirement accounts were tightly regulated, some investors would succumb to sharp sales practices, and marketing costs would eat up a substantial portion of the returns. Experience in the United Kingdom supports such concerns.[9] Even with extensive protections, individuals would be exposed to the risks of fluctuations in interest rates and asset prices that can undermine the adequacy of what once looked like a sufficient nest egg (see Figure 3–1).

LABOR MARKET EFFICIENCY

Advocates of personal accounts claim that a privatized system would distort workers' decisions about how much to work less than Social Security does. They argue that workers are well aware of the payroll taxes they must pay, but have little understanding of, and therefore place little value on, the benefits they will ultimately receive in return for these payments. Thus, the system as a whole is perceived primarily as a tax that, like other taxes on earnings, distorts labor supply by reducing the returns workers think they receive for additional work effort. Distortions under a privatized system, they feel, would be smaller because workers would better understand, and feel more secure about, the benefits that contributions to their retirement accounts finance.

This argument is somewhat oversimplified. The same myopia that makes mandatory saving desirable will cause workers to undervalue future benefits from individual accounts just as they do Social Security benefits. Nevertheless, it is possible that labor supply could be affected differently if workers have a greater appreciation of the benefits they hope to receive from their personal accounts than of those they will receive from Social Security. However, to the extent that misunderstanding is the problem, education, not privatization, is the answer.

The principal difference in work incentives between a privatized system and Social Security arises from variations in the social assistance each system might provide. Apart from administrative cost differences that would favor Social Security, the benefits per dollar of taxes paid, on average, would be the same under the two systems, if reserves are similarly invested. But income redistribution necessarily entails taxing some people to provide assistance to others. The labor supply distortions that arise from taxes and transfers are an inescapable price of social assistance. The more social assistance—for low earners, large families, nonworking spouses, and widows and widowers—the more the distortions. If the effects on labor supply of Social Security vary from those of a privatized system, the differences arise either from lack of information or from differences in real social assistance.

INCREASED NATIONAL SAVING

The primary benefit claimed for privatization is that it would boost national saving. As we emphasized in Chapter 4, the case for raising national saving is strong. Increased saving, and the higher rate of capital formation that this saving would generate, would boost the growth of output per worker and help the nation shoulder the costs of a gradually increasing dependent population. Replacing a partially funded Social Security system with fully funded private accounts would probably boost national saving. But so too would a buildup of Social Security reserves.

Which approach would raise saving more? The answer, alas, is a resounding: Nobody knows! To explain why this is the case, we must examine the three conditions that determine how much new saving would result from a dollar added to the Social Security trust funds' reserves and a dollar deposited in a personal retirement account—the yields, budget offsets, and private offsets.

Yields. If the choice is between contributions to personal retirement accounts and equal additions to Social Security reserves, the one that has the higher yield will grow fastest and tend to add more to saving since all the contributions and investment returns accumulated in the two are held until paid out as pensions.[10] Current law requires Social Security to invest its reserves only in securities guaranteed as to principal and interest by the government.[11] Because Treasury securities are free of default risk, they tend to yield less than the assets held by private pension funds—corporate bonds, stocks, and real estate. In other words, yield differences arise from restrictions imposed on the trust funds' managers, and have nothing to do with privatization. If Social Security could invest its additional reserves in the same assets private fund managers normally select, it would earn similar returns and generate as much saving.

Budget Offsets. Any increase in government spending or cut in taxes stimulated by the buildup of Social Security reserves would reduce the effect of accumulation of the trust funds on national saving (see Box 5–1, page 84). To the extent that buildup in the trust funds does not trigger tax cuts or spending increases, additions to Social Security reserves boost national saving by raising budget surpluses or reducing deficits. Starting in 1986, the Social Security system was officially "off-budget." But official documents continued to focus on the unified budget, which includes Social Security. In the 1998 State of the Union address, President Clinton urged that the prospective unified budget surpluses be preserved until legislation restoring financial balance in Social Security had been enacted. During 1999, a bipartisan consensus developed that surpluses accumulating in the Social Security trust funds should not be used for either tax cuts or spending increases. This consensus was expressed as a shift in the nation's fiscal policy goal—from balance in the "unified budget," which encompasses all operations of government, including Social Security, to balance in the budget excluding Social Security. Continuing to keep the operations of Social Security separate from other budget accounts in official documents and in policy debates involving other tax and expenditure decisions would buttress this commitment and increase the likelihood that any reserve

---

BOX 5–1
THE ABCS OF NATIONAL SAVING

National saving is the difference between what the nation produces and what it consumes, publicly and privately. It consists of real resources that are available for investment in new office buildings and stores, industrial plants, warehouses, equipment, inventories, and residential structures. It is this real capital that adds to national productivity. Certificates of ownership—common stocks, bonds, mortgages, mutual fund shares, royalty contracts—are the counterparts of this real capital, but do not themselves add a scintilla to economic capacity. It is *real* capital that counts, not the value of *paper* capital.

To understand how an increase in funding of pensions can raise national saving, it helps to divide total national saving (NS) into four components: private saving for retirement (P_{RS}), private saving for other purposes (P_O), government saving under Social Security (G_{SS}), and government saving in the rest of its operations (G_O).

$$NS = P_{RS} + P_O + G_{SS} + G_O$$

Social Security surpluses increase trust fund reserves and raise G_{SS}. This will not raise national saving, however, if elected officials use Social Security reserves to underwrite equal increases in deficits (or reductions in surpluses) on other operations of government, which would show up as a decline in G_O. Mandatory private retirement saving will boost P_{RS}, but this will not raise national saving if people cut back on other forms of saving, P_O, equally. The effect on national saving of adding the same amount to P_{RS} or to G_{SS} will be identical as long as the offsets to P_O and G_O are the same.

The central question in the debate about whether accumulating reserves in Social Security (that is, adding to G_{SS}) or in personal retirement accounts (that is, adding to P_{RS}) will add more to national saving boils down to whether the offsets in P_O or in G_O will be larger.

---

accumulation would boost saving. In Chapter 6 we describe ways to promote this goal.

Private Offsets. The creation of personal retirement accounts could either raise or lower other household saving. Personal retirement accounts might advertise the virtues of saving and thereby increase it. Business-sponsored programs to explain their 401(k) pension plans have raised saving.[12] They advertise the advantages of saving, showing that repeated deposits, even small ones, can grow to significant balances over time. These programs foster a climate in which saving is respected and valued. Periodic statements of personal account balances could also demonstrate the power of compound investment returns. Such reports, together with reminders about the dangers of saving too little, can teach frugality and lead workers to save more outside their personal retirement accounts. Of course, one does not need to privatize Social Security to undertake private and public campaigns to educate workers on the virtues of saving.

While this "consciousness-raising" argument carries some force, the bulk of economic research suggests that growing balances in private accounts would tend to raise consumption—that is, lower saving—because asset owners feel wealthier. Most people now express great skepticism that they will receive all the Social Security benefits current law promises. If they receive a periodic statement showing that their very own personal retirement account balances are large and rising, they are likely to feel more secure about their retirement incomes, raise consumption, and reduce other saving.

Thus, creating private retirement accounts would probably reduce other saving. How much is unclear. Experience with tax provisions designed to encourage retirement saving is worrisome. After Congress created tax incentives, like IRAs, to promote individual retirement saving, saving in tax-sheltered individual accounts rose from nothing to 1 percent of disposable income during the 1990–94 period. Unfortunately, voluntary saving, apart from retirement saving and life insurance, fell from 7.9 percent of disposable income in the 1970s to 2.9 percent from 1990 to 1994 and then vanished entirely in 1997–98.[13] While many factors other than the advent of tax-sheltered saving influenced private saving during this period, one cannot escape the troubling possibility that many people may have just shifted assets and saving from taxable accounts to the new tax-sheltered vehicles. This episode serves as a warning: If people are forced to save in one form they may cut back in another.

It is impossible to forecast reliably the net effect of these various incentives and offsets. Replacement of the government's largest program, one that provides most retirees with most of their income, is bound to have unforeseen consequences. But one effect is likely—accumulating pension reserves should raise national saving somewhat, whether reserves are held in Social Security trust funds or personal retirement accounts. Which form of reserve accumulation will raise saving more is impossible to predict because the results depend sensitively on plan details and on behaviors—of private individuals and elected officials—that no one can reliably predict.

POLITICAL CONFLICT

The specter of intergenerational conflict has been much in the news in recent years. Some people fear an ugly political scrum between greedy geezers struggling to hold on to their benefits and beleaguered workers fighting to protect themselves and their families from onerous taxes. It is hard to know how seriously to take such apprehensions. Opinion polls report that young and middle-aged adults strongly support Social Security and Medicare, even as they voice concern over whether these programs will actually deliver benefits promised to them. The young are almost as likely as the elderly to feel that these programs should be enriched as that they should be cut back.[14] Elderly and disabled beneficiaries are, after all, the siblings, parents, and grandparents of active workers who care not only about their taxes but also about the continued financial security of their relatives.

Privatization could eventually end the potential for intergenerational conflict over Social Security taxes and benefits because each generation would pay fully for its own retirement. This advantage, however, would be slow in coming. For several decades, in fact, privatization could intensify intergenerational conflict. Young workers might well resent the burden of paying for two retirement pensions— one for previous generations of workers who would be receiving diminished Social Security benefits and one for themselves through their own retirement accounts. Some young workers might wonder why they should be carrying such burdens, especially when some of the benefits for retirees would be going to people with significant private pensions and asset income. Of course, the same feelings could develop if Social Security moved to a more fully funded system.

Updating Contribution Rates. Privatization would raise new and potentially divisive issues for public discussion. Instead of debating whether to impose added taxes on workers or to cut benefits, people would argue over how much people should be required to contribute to their own accounts. If contribution rates were held constant, changes in wage growth, asset values, and interest rates could substantially change replacement rates, as we illustrated in Chapter 3. To prevent such large fluctuations, sizable adjustments would have to be made periodically in the required individual contribution rate. And when asset prices fell, Congress would come under pressure to compensate those who were about to retire for their losses (see Box 5–2 for a past example of such pressures).

Box 5–2
The Peculiar Politics of "Notch Babies"

Before 1975, Social Security benefits were not automatically adjusted for inflation. Instead, Congress periodically passed legislation to offset the effects of inflation. Doing so took time and bother, but it had its reward—voters were grateful. Not surprisingly, bills to raise Social Security benefits were enacted mostly just before congressional elections. Democrats controlled Congress and got most of the credit. Republicans steamed. Partly to eliminate this opportunity for political advantage, Republicans urged that benefits be automatically adjusted for inflation. The proposal was clearly a good idea on substantive grounds. By the 1970s, inflation was becoming more of a problem than it had been since World War II. Why make the retired and disabled wait until Congress got around to acting? With bipartisan support, legislation was passed in 1972 that raised benefits by a whopping 20 percent and called for automatic "indexation" of Social Security starting in 1975.

Unfortunately, the adjustment formula Congress adopted was flawed. Congress was not at fault. The formula was the same one the actuaries had used in the past to design ad hoc legislated increases. It worked well enough when inflation was low, but provided excessive adjustments when inflation was high. When inflation was more than 1 to 2 percent, as it was with disturbing consistency during the 1970s, replacement rates—the ratio of benefits to average wages—rose relentlessly. For the average earner, replacement rates rose from 34 percent in 1970 to a peak of 54 percent for those who turned 62 in 1978. But payroll tax receipts rose no faster than average wages, and deficits began to develop.

Something had to be done. The Carter administration proposed a formula that adjusted benefits correctly for inflation and called on Congress to reduce replacement rates for people who reached retirement age *after* 1977 to what they would have been if the inflation adjustment had been made correctly all along. But it did not propose, and Congress did not enact, any change in benefits for those who had reached retirement age *between* 1972 and 1977 and had benefited from the flawed indexation mechanism.

This decision spared Congress one problem—the need to take benefits away from people who already had reached retirement age. But it created another—a "notch." Benefits were approximately 10 percent smaller on the average for people who reached retirement age just after 1977 than for those who reached retirement just before. Those affected adversely came to be known as the "notch babies." The exact differential between their benefits and those of people who became eligible just before 1977 depended on individual circumstances. But, whatever the differential, those on the short end felt shortchanged. They formed protest clubs. They filled congressional mailbags with letters venting outrage. Commissions were established to analyze the problem. Congressional committees held hearings. Members introduced "corrective" legislation. Not surprisingly, only two of the 113 "corrective" bills would have lowered the erroneous excess benefits paid to those born before 1917. The others would have raised the correctly calculated benefits of those born after 1916.

Continued on the next page

BOX 5–2 (CONTINUED)
THE PECULIAR POLITICS OF "NOTCH BABIES"

In the end, Congress resisted the protests of the notch babies. Privately, many members understood that the case for raising benefits for the notch babies was insubstantial. Outside organizations, including a blue-ribbon panel created by the National Academy of Social Insurance, made clear that the claims of the notch babies were unjustified. And budget pressures made any expenditure increases hard to justify. In the end, Congress left the 1977 legislation alone. But the furor created over the 10 percent benefit differential that arose from the flawed adjustment formula serves as a warning of the problems that might arise if price fluctuations in financial markets cause even larger benefit differentials under a privatized system.

The problem can be illustrated by examining the changes in contribution rates that would have been required under a hypothetical defined-contribution retirement plan that started operations in 1953 and was designed to provide pensions that replaced half of pre-retirement earnings. If the contribution rate was adjusted once each decade to keep the plan headed for that 50 percent replacement rate, contributions would have varied from a low of 5.2 percent to a high of 39 percent of earnings.[15] With less frequent adjustments, pensions would have fallen well short of or greatly exceeded the target replacement rate. This analysis does not reflect the sharp variations in asset values that occur within and between years, described in Chapter 3, which would have caused replacement rates for workers reaching retirement age just a few months or years apart to differ greatly.

Government-guaranteed investment returns or minimum benefits could protect defined-contribution pensioners from stock or bond market crashes and from imprudent investments. Such protections would probably be subject to a means test to limit costs and to focus assistance on the truly needy. Without such limits, investment protection would create perverse incentives for workers to pursue excessively risky investment strategies, safe in the knowledge that they could keep high returns while the government, in effect, insured them against loss. Means tests increase complexity and administrative costs. In addition, a guarantee would have to be financed by raising taxes or cutting other government spending, measures that would raise intergenerational tensions similar to those allegedly facing Social Security.

Social Adequacy. One of the major current functions of Social Security is the provision of economic assistance to retirees with a history of low earnings. This Social Security benefit formula provides such assistance automatically by generating higher "replacement rates" for low earners. Such income redistribution is likely to become a more divisive issue under a privatized system than it is today. Some privatization plans maintain benefits for low earners through a separate component in a dual system. For example, under one plan, retired workers who had been employed a minimum number of years would receive a flat benefit financed by payroll taxes, in addition to a pension derived from personal retirement accounts that were financed by mandatory individual deposits. The combination could approximate the distribution of benefits under the current system. However, all the redistribution would be concentrated in the flat benefit component. As the ratio of retirees to active workers increases, the payroll tax rate required to support the flat benefit would increase, raising pressures similar to those that some feel will lead to generational warfare if the current Social Security system is maintained. Creating a dual system does nothing to reduce this source of potential intergenerational conflict. It would simply focus this tension on the component of the new system that disproportionately serves low earners.

To sum up, replacing Social Security with a system of individual accounts would change, but not necessarily cool, debate about retirement policy. Pensions are so costly to society and so important to the elderly, disabled, and survivors that political debate on retirement policy will always be intense. Privatization would eventually end debates over how to close the projected deficits in the partially funded Social Security system because the benefit obligations of defined-contribution plans are limited to accumulated reserves in personal retirement accounts. But other contentious issues would remain. What compensation, if any, would be provided to retirees who end up with inadequate pensions because of bad investment decisions or downturns in financial markets? Who should pay for the costs of transition to the new system? What, if anything, should be done to sustain the retirement incomes of low-wage workers whose personal security accounts provide insufficient benefits?

Risks of Privatization

A switch from Social Security to privatized personal retirement accounts carries a number of risks. We have already described several. Poor investment returns could leave some cohorts of workers and some workers within each cohort with inadequate pensions. Variations in investment returns would assuredly produce large variations in pensions among people who had made similar contributions. Unanticipated inflation could erode the value of pensions of older retirees. Political support for the crucial antipoverty role that Social Security has played for more than a half-century could atrophy. Two other problems associated with privatization deserve more attention—administrative costs and individual ignorance about financial markets.

Administrative Costs

All pension plans, public or private, must collect and keep track of individual workers' contributions, distribute information to participants, manage assets, determine eligibility for benefits, and pay retirement benefits. Expenditures to perform these tasks unavoidably reduce the growth of account balances and should therefore be kept as low as possible, consistent with adequate service.

The Social Security Administration (SSA) sets a high standard for administrative efficiency and customer service. The total cost of administering Social Security retirement and survivor's insurance runs about 0.6 percent of benefit payments.[16] SSA enjoys economies of scale that private plans cannot match. Practically all of SSA's costs go for clerical functions—keeping track of individuals' earnings, distributing reports to participants, and paying benefits.[17] A small amount represents the costs the Treasury Department incurs collecting payroll taxes. Private employers incur few extra costs collecting and remitting the Social Security payroll taxes because they must keep track of workers' earnings anyway to compute business and personal income, Medicare, and unemployment compensation taxes.

Running a system of personal retirement accounts would be more expensive than running Social Security. How much more expensive depends on the type of plan. The principal extra administrative costs of privatized alternatives arise from selling expenses, costs for managing assets, costs for verifying the accuracy of records, and profits for private companies carrying out these tasks. Social Security incurs no selling costs because the plan is universal and mandatory. The cost of managing the trust funds' reserves is also trivial because the balances in the Social Security trust funds are invested centrally only in securities guaranteed as to principal and interest by the U.S. government. And verification costs are limited because earnings credits are linked to wages reported for income tax purposes. In addition, because Social Security benefits depend only on average earnings, which are calculated once at age 60, errors are relatively easy to correct. In contrast, each deposit in personal accounts would have to be verified because errors in credits would compound over time.

The 1997 Advisory Council on Social Security estimated that costs for individually managed plans that would permit people to invest freely in stocks, bonds, or mutual funds, as well as in investment products offered by insurance companies or brokerage houses, would average 1 percent of funds managed per year. *Such an annual charge is equivalent to a front-end loading charge of about 20 percent.* Plans that allowed workers to designate various funds in which their deposits should be credited also would impose increased administrative costs on employers. In contrast to Social Security, which requires employers simply to forward payroll tax contributions to the Treasury, along with other taxes that would have to be paid anyway, employers would have to remit funds directly to a number of different financial intermediaries rather than send a single check to the Treasury.

Small businesses and companies employing low-wage workers would be especially burdened. The 5.4 million employers that do not use computerized payroll systems would find it costly to make timely deposits into their workers' various investment accounts. Moreover, many of these deposits would be small. If 2 percent of earnings were designated for personal retirement accounts and each worker maintained only one account, half of the deposits employers would make each month would be less than $31 and one-fifth would be less than $9. Relative to the amounts involved, employer and financial institution administrative costs would be high. Finally, if workers in such a plan could choose whether to convert fund balances into annuities, they would face an additional charge that is estimated to average between 10 and 20 percent of the price of the annuity.[18]

Not all privatization plans would involve such high administrative costs. The 1996 Advisory Council on Social Security estimated that government-managed plans modeled after the federal employees' Thrift Savings Plan (TSP) would have annual costs close to those of the TSP—that is, about 0.105 percent of funds managed. Initially, the TSP permitted participants to invest only in three funds managed passively to minimize administrative costs. Starting in May 2001, the TSP program will add two index funds—one that tracks small companies and one for international stocks. The initial menu included index funds that track short-term government securities, longer-term private and government debt instruments, and the S&P 500 stock index. Several factors suggest that administrative costs of a plan with similar rules covering all nongovernment workers would be considerably higher. The TSP deals with only federal agencies, all of which are computerized, not with millions of small and large employers. These agencies, not TSP, provide many account services and education. Job turnover in the federal government is low compared to that of the private sector. Wages, and thus contribution amounts, are relatively high. In addition, federal personnel records contain family information that a pension plan would need in case workers got divorced.[19]

Nonetheless, costs for this type of plan would be substantially lower than those for plans that let workers choose among a lengthy menu of investment options. A TSP-type plan would limit investment choice to a small number of passively managed, no-load index funds—such as a stock market index fund, a corporate bond index fund, and a government bond fund. A few financial institutions would be selected through competitive bids to manage investments. The government would prohibit the management firms from attempting to influence investors' choices through aggressive selling or advertising, and account balances would have to be paid as indexed annuities upon retirement. Such a centralized system of individual accounts would capture many of the economies of scale in administration enjoyed by Social Security today.

A system of individually managed accounts could bring huge revenues to the financial services industry. The initial annual flow of investment funds into a privatized system that channeled 2 percent of earnings into private accounts would be about $79 billion. If administrative costs average 1 percent of accumulated funds, the annual revenue from managing these funds would grow to $14 billion after ten years and rise steadily thereafter. Nonetheless, it is unclear whether this business would be profitable. Small accounts are costly to administer. Any whiff of scandal would bring congressional hearings and federal regulation that may well affect the other operations of the financial industry.

Any comparison of administrative costs should encompass the whole system. Social Security's administrative structure handles three categories of benefits—retirement pensions, survivor's benefits, and disability payments. This arrangement provides economies of scope—one agency for three programs—and of scale—154 million insured workers and 45 million beneficiaries. Privatization plans would necessarily duplicate administrative structures and costs because most privatization plans would retain Social Security retirement benefits for at least several decades and continue survivor's and disability insurance permanently.

PERSONAL CONTROL OVER ACCOUNTS

Advocates of privatization lay particular stress on the value of individual control of personal retirement accounts, both before and after retirement. With individual control, however, come important economic and political problems. If individuals own identified personal accounts and are free to determine how these funds are invested, they are likely to regard these accounts as personal property similar to other personal saving. Pressure will build to allow withdrawals before retirement.

The experience with IRAs is instructive. Originally, nearly all IRA withdrawals made before age $59^{1}/_2$ were subject both to regular income tax and to a 10 percent penalty tax. In 1996, the law was changed to permit penalty-free withdrawals to meet large medical expenses and to buy health insurance if the account holder was unemployed. The Taxpayers Relief Act of 1997 liberalized the law further by permitting penalty-free withdrawals to cover expenses associated with the purchase of a first home and for postsecondary educational expenses of a family member. Similar arguments would be made under a privatized system—that account holders should be allowed to withdraw funds from their retirement accounts to pay for personal health care expenses if they or a family member is seriously ill, to pay educational expenses, and for other purposes. As restrictions are relaxed, it becomes more likely that some, possibly many, workers will draw down their personal account balances before retirement, defeating the very purpose of the accounts and exposing the government to larger future welfare payments to retirees who have depleted their accounts and become indigent.

The discretion that people are given over the use of their personal accounts at retirement is also problematic in a program to assure a basic retirement income. While some privatization proposals would require workers to convert account balances into annuities at retirement, others would permit people to withdraw funds in a lump sum when they retire or in a series of payments spread over several years. Still other plans would allow those who can support themselves in retirement with other resources to leave their fund balances on deposit and bequeath them to their heirs at death. Because of adverse selection, giving people an option not to annuitize boosts prices for those who want annuities. To combat this risk, insurers must offer smaller annuities to everyone than would be possible if annuitization were mandatory.[20]

If annuitization were optional, some people would exhaust their savings and become public charges. In addition, people whose annuities would approximate the aggregate benefits from Supplemental Security Income benefits, food stamps, and other means-tested programs would face a perverse incentive not to annuitize. Instead, they could withdraw their savings over a few years, during which they could enjoy an elevated standard of living. After their savings were exhausted, they could fall back on welfare, where they would enjoy about the same income an annuity would have provided.

If people could hold their personal accounts until they die, so-called *retirement* accounts would become little more than devices people could use to escape taxes on investment income and to build their estates for their heirs. This feature would help only the wealthy.

PRIVATIZATION—A SUMMING UP

Converting Social Security retirement benefits to personal retirement accounts means replacing a defined-benefit pension system with a defined-contribution pension system. This shift would place on individual retirees a variety of financial market risks that Social Security now diffuses broadly across workers and taxpayers, both current and future. We believe that individuals are poorly equipped to handle these risks and that a defined-benefit pension should continue to serve as the source of the nation's basic retirement pensions.

On the other hand, reserve accumulation in private accounts or in expanded Social Security trust funds could increase U.S. saving rates. Forcing the baby-boom generation, now in its prime working years, to shoulder a part of the burden of building these reserves would enrich the nation's capital stock, raise worker productivity, and offset some of the costs future workers will bear to support the baby boomers.

A system of supplementary personal retirement saving could also be used to build up reserves. If such a course were followed, the new program should be additional to a basic defined-benefit pension, such as Social Security. For reasons we shall explain in the next chapter, we can see no compelling case for scaling back Social Security benefits to "make room" for a supplementary system. Such "carve-out" plans would cut assured benefits that are by no means generous to make room for supplementary benefits that force workers and pensioners to shoulder more risk and would raise administrative costs. Whatever the size of a new program of mandatory personal saving, rules should restrict investments to no-load index funds managed in a manner similar to the Thrift Savings Plan of federal employees. The average returns on funds as large as those of any mandatory saving program cannot deviate much from the market-wide average rate of return. Since nothing can significantly boost this return, anything spent on administration, beyond the bare minimum necessary for speedy investment, is pure waste and should be avoided. Enriching pensioners, not financial institutions, should be the objective of pension reform.

6

THE CASE FOR PRESERVING
SOCIAL SECURITY: HOW
SHOULD IT BE DONE?

From small beginnings, Social Security has become the largest and most popular program of the federal government. Its benefits account for 5.3 percent of the nation's personal income, more than half of the income for 58 percent of the elderly, and more than 90 percent of the income for more than one-quarter of the elderly. Because of Social Security, millions of older workers can now afford to retire while still active and healthy. The program's financial support allows most retired and disabled people to live modestly but independently. It thereby spares beneficiaries the indignity of becoming financially dependent on government welfare, private charity, or their children. It spares millions of nonelderly the burden of supporting dependent relatives. Because benefits are provided as inflation-protected annuities, recipients need not worry that market fluctuations, inflation, or an especially long life will rob them of their financial independence. Without much controversy, Social Security has become the government's most powerful antipoverty policy. Without its benefits, 48 percent of the elderly would be poor; with these benefits, only 9 percent are.[1]

Although Social Security is important and successful, even its most ardent supporters acknowledge that the program has shortcomings. In some respects, Social Security reflects the economic, social, and demographic conditions of a past age. A modernized and strengthened Social Security system, not the existing one, should be the program compared to the fully or partially privatized approaches that have been proposed as replacements for the current Social Security system.

Of the many changes, small and large, that could strengthen and modernize the program's benefit structure and financing, the most important are:

◆   to modify benefits provided to spouses in recognition of the increased labor force participation of women;

◆   to improve the adequacy of benefits for older survivors;

◆   to make the annual cost-of-living adjustments more accurate;

◆   to increase the age of initial eligibility for retirement benefits, in recognition of the improved health and longevity of the elderly;

◆   to transfer some of the costs of the unfunded liability from future workers to the general taxpayer; and

◆   to speed the accumulation of financial reserves and diversify the assets in which Social Security reserves are invested.

Taken together, the changes would restore and sustain the approximate long-run balance between the system's revenues and expenditures for the seventy-five-year official projection period and beyond.

STRENGTHS OF THE CURRENT SYSTEM

Before describing ways to strengthen the existing system, we review four attributes of Social Security that privatization could jeopardize but that we feel are particularly important to preserve.

SOCIAL ASSISTANCE

Preservation of Social Security's financial assistance to low earners and other vulnerable participants is vital. Such assistance ensures that low earners receive benefits sufficient to sustain financial independence in retirement. Compared either to benefits abroad or to domestic measures of income adequacy, pensions provided by the current system are far from generous (see Box 6–1). For workers with average earnings, the U.S. replacement rate is less than half those of the French and Dutch systems and less than two-thirds of those offered by the Belgian, Italian, German, and Spanish systems. Overall, the replacement rate for early retirees in

---

BOX 6–1
THE BENEFIT FORMULA

Social Security replaces more of the pay of low earners than of high earners because it provides a larger payback on their first few thousand dollars of average earnings than on higher amounts. For example, benefits for workers who will claim benefits at age 65 in the year 2003 will equal 90 percent of annual earnings up to $6,372, 32 percent of annual earnings from $6,372 to $38,424, and 15 percent of annual earnings from $38,424 to $76,200, the maximum earnings subject to payroll taxes in 2000 when these workers turned age 62.

Each year the maximum earnings subject to tax and the income ranges used in the benefit formula are raised by the growth in average earnings in jobs covered by Social Security. Between 1999 and 2000, for example, the top of the 90 percent range rose from $6,060 to $6,372, a 5.1 percent increase. The following annual pension amounts and replacement rates illustrate how the benefit formula worked in 2000 for those retiring at age 65 after working at least 35 years at various earnings levels.

Average Adjusted Earnings	Annual Pension (Dollars)	Replacement Rate (Percent)
Low Earnings—45 percent of the average wage ($11,292)	$ 7,176	64
Average wage ($25,092)	11,844	47
High Earnings—160 percent of the average wage ($38,268)	15,348	40
Maximum taxable earnings ($49,932)	17,196	34

the United States ranked tenth among eleven nations examined in one study, even though the United States had the highest age of initial eligibility.[2]

Compared to official U.S. poverty thresholds, benefits are parsimonious. A worker retiring in 1999 after a lifetime of year-round work at the minimum wage received a pension that was slightly under the poverty threshold for a single person; a minimum-wage married retiree received a benefit that was just above the poverty threshold for a couple.[3] Benefits of average earners are less than 1.5 times the poverty threshold if they start drawing benefits at age 65, and are only 14 percent over the poverty threshold if they start benefits at age 62. If pensions were proportional to earnings or payroll tax payments, benefits for low earners would fall by over 25 percent. Poverty among the elderly, disabled, and survivors would increase. Welfare expenditures would rise. And many young and middle-aged workers would have to support parents, siblings, and other relatives who now manage independently.

The current benefit rules of the Social Security system favor not only low earners but also survivors, spouses, and divorcees who have had no or limited earnings. Later in this chapter, we describe desirable modifications in the benefits available to these groups.

A completely privatized system cannot offer these forms of assistance. To sustain extra benefits for vulnerable groups, a separate government program would be necessary. Placing social assistance in a distinct program would destroy the integration of pensions and social assistance, which lies at the heart of Social Security. The social assistance program could come to be regarded as welfare, a category of government spending that has had little sustained political support in the United States.

INFLATION PROTECTION

Inflation protection is a second important aspect of Social Security that should be preserved. Among the nation's pension programs, only Social Security benefits are raised annually to compensate fully for price increases over the previous year.[4] In the past, no major private pension plan offered comparable protection. Because long-run inflation is unpredictable, the financial risks of guaranteeing inflation-protected "real" annuities could have bankrupted even the strongest private insurers before 1997, when the Treasury began to issue "indexed" securities—bonds that pay a fixed interest yield, plus compensation for the inflation that has occurred over the previous year. This innovation has made it possible for private insurance companies to offer real annuities backed up by government index bonds, but none has yet done so. As a result, Social Security remains the only source of retirement income fully insulated from the risk of unanticipated inflation and guaranteed to last as long as the pensioners live.[5]

WAGE RISK

Because Social Security benefits vary less than proportionately with earnings, they provide a kind of insurance against the consequences of low earnings. Furthermore, benefits depend on a worker's average lifetime earnings, not on when the worker receives the earnings. Year-to-year earnings may differ, depending on the duration of education, mid-career breaks to raise children, and spells of unemployment. But workers with the same earnings averaged over their lifetimes receive the same Social Security benefits.

FINANCIAL MARKET PROTECTION

Pension benefits depend on the returns earned on accumulated reserves. If returns fall short of expectations, contributions have to increase or benefits have to be cut. But whose contributions and whose benefits? Fluctuations in returns under individual accounts fall entirely on the worker who owns the individual account. Under Social Security, in contrast, higher or lower than anticipated returns result in small benefit adjustments or tax changes that are spread among current and future workers and pensioners. Since the function of social insurance is to ensure basic income, linking pensions to stable quantities, such as a worker's lifetime earnings, is important. While it also is desirable to invest pension reserves so that they yield high returns—and we indicate below ways to manage investment of a diversified Social Security portfolio—it is vital to make sure that risks of market fluctuations are broadly shared and not borne by individual pensioners.

STRENGTHENING SOCIAL SECURITY
FOR THE FUTURE

Although Social Security is projected to run cash-flow surpluses of $172 billion to $274 billion a year for the next decade, the system faces a projected long-term deficit. Because changes in the system should be introduced gradually, it is desirable to close that deficit well before cash-flow surpluses end. In this chapter, we present a menu of steps that would restore financial balance for the next seventy-five years and beyond (see Table 6–1). These changes would not alter the fundamental structure of Social Security. But adopting all would create sizable projected long-term *surpluses*. This menu illustrates why the added costs of pensions for the baby-boom generation should not be offered as justification for radical changes in the structure of the nation's basic pension system.

The items in the menu are divided into two broad categories: changes in benefits or in the computation of benefits and changes in revenues. The menu does not include any increase in either the payroll tax rate or the earnings base.

SPOUSE'S AND SURVIVOR'S BENEFITS

Social Security has always provided all workers, men and women alike, benefits based on their own earnings. In 1939, one year before the first worker's benefits were paid, Congress added a spouse's benefit set at half of the primary worker's benefit for wives or husbands who had no or limited lifetime earnings. This provision results in larger benefits for retired couples than for single retirees. It dates from an era when most married women stayed home to care for children. For many years, most married women received the spouse's benefit because few had sufficient earnings to qualify them for a larger worker's benefit. Now, far more women receive retirement benefits based on their own earnings than receive spouse's benefits—13.3 million versus 2.8 million at the end of 1998.

The increasing likelihood that both spouses work has interacted with the benefit formula to create two problems. The first is the so-called lesser-earner problem. The spouse with the lower earnings—usually the wife—owes payroll taxes from the first dollar of earnings and becomes entitled to benefits after forty quarters of covered work.

Table 6–1
Closing the Projected Long-term
Social Security Deficit

	Deficit or Change in Deficit as Percentage of Payroll	Proportion of Long-term Deficit Closed
Projected long-term deficit— 2000 Trustees Report	−1.89	n.a.
Benefit Changes		
1. Gradually reduce spouse's benefits from one-half to one-third of the worker's benefits and raise benefits for surviving spouses to three-quarters of the couple's combined benefit.	−0.03	−2
2. Cut benefits by increasing the unreduced benefit age—raise the age to 67 by 2011, rather than by 2022, and thereafter raise the age at which unreduced benefits are paid to hold constant the fraction of adult life spent in retirement.	+0.52	28
3. Increase the age of initial eligibility from 62 to 64 by 2011; thereafter raise the age of initial eligibility at the same pace as the unreduced benefits age.	+0.18	10
4. Increase the period over which earnings are averaged from thirty-five to thirty-eight years.	+0.25	13
5. Cover all newly hired state and local employees.	+0.21	11
6. Tax Social Security benefits like contributory private pension income.	+0.42	22
Total Benefit Changes (including interactions)	**+1.49**	**79**
Financing Changes		
1. Transfer general revenue to pay off the unfunded liability.	+0.96	51
2. Invest up to 20 percent of reserves in common stocks; also, invest in bonds of FNMA and government agencies	+0.42	22
Total Financing Changes	**+1.38**	**73**
Total Program Changes	**+2.87**	**152**

Source: Estimates from the Office of the Actuary, Social Security Administration.

However, retirement benefits for a two-earner couple exceed those of a one-earner couple only when the lesser earner's benefit exceeds half of the principal earner's benefit.[6] Even then, the benefit increment above the spouse's benefit is small relative to the payroll taxes they have contributed to the system (see Box 6–2). This arrangement favors married women (or men) who do not work for pay. It does not discriminate against workers of either sex because all are entitled to benefits based on their own earnings records.

Eliminating the Spouse's Benefit. The simplest and least costly way to end the lesser-earner problem would be to eliminate the spouse's benefit altogether. However, this step would significantly reduce benefits for the many older couples in which one spouse worked outside the home little or not at all. It would also make it far more costly for one parent to stay home to care for the children. But a large majority of mothers, even those with preschool children, now work, and that proportion has been rising. To aid parents who remain at home to care for children, Vice President Al Gore proposed as part of his 2000 campaign for president to give earnings credits of one-half of the average wage for up to five years spent caring for young children. Such a provision would further reduce the need for the spouse's benefit. A gradual reduction in the spouse's benefit over a decade or so from one-half of the principal earner's benefit to one-third or even one-quarter would free up funds that could be used to lower the projected long-term deficit or applied to improving benefits in other ways.[7]

Earnings Sharing. Some observers favor a more far-reaching change called "earnings sharing." Earnings of a couple would be pooled, and each spouse would be credited with half of the total.[8] Since both spouses would have an earnings history, there would be no need for a separate spouse's benefit. Earnings sharing would protect divorced spouses who earned little outside the home and whose marriages did not last at least a decade, the period necessary under current law for divorcees to receive benefits based on their former spouse's earnings record.[9] Nearly one-third of all marriages end in divorce in less than ten years.

Earnings sharing would lower benefits for many and could create difficulties for some. In one-earner couples, retirement might be difficult until both spouses were old enough to qualify for pensions, since the pension of the primary earner would be reduced by shifting some of his or her earnings to the lesser earner. Where the primary

Box 6–2
The Spouse's Benefit

Four couples, the Campbells, the Steins, the Smiths, and the Joneses, live in the same neighborhood. The husbands were all born in 1937 and have held similar jobs at the local factory where each earned, over his lifetime, the average worker's wage. In 2002, they turn age 65 and retire. Each husband receives a Social Security retirement benefit of $987 per month.

Sally Campbell has raised her children, taken care of her sick mother-in-law, and been an active volunteer at the church and Girl Scouts. But she never worked in the paid labor force. When her husband retires, she is entitled to a spouse's benefit of $493, one-half of her husband's benefit.

Judy Stein worked a bit before she had children and then dropped out of the paid workforce for several decades to raise her family and participate on the town council. She then worked part-time for a decade. Her earnings experience entitles her to a worker's benefit equal to 20 percent of her husband's benefit. Because this is less than the amount available under the spouse's benefit, she also receives a reduced spouse's benefit sufficient to bring her total benefit up to one-half of her husband's benefit. She and her husband have paid a bit more in Social Security taxes than the Campbells, but their overall benefits are the same.

Charlotte Smith raised her children while holding down a part-time job. She went back to work full-time when the youngest left for college. Her average lifetime earnings, however, amounted to only 29 percent of her husband's earnings. Although she earned considerably less than half of what her husband earned, she is entitled to a retirement benefit equal to half of her husband's benefit. Although she and her husband have paid considerably more in payroll taxes into the system than have the Campbells, the benefits they receive are no larger.

Ruth Jones took a travel agency job just after leaving school and enjoyed it so much that she worked steadily full-time even while raising her children. Her average lifetime earnings and payroll tax payments equaled her husband's. As a result, she receives a retirement pension equal to her husband's. But while the Joneses have contributed twice as much to the Social Security system over the years as have the Campbells, their combined benefit is only one-third larger.

These examples illustrate the following facts:

1. Social Security treats couples at least as generously as it treats two single people with the same earnings.

2. The spouse's benefit is paid even if one spouse does not work at all.

3. Social Security does not discriminate against lesser-earning spouses, most of whom are women. It discriminates in favor of the lesser earner (usually the woman) by paying a benefit equal to half of the primary earner's (usually the man) benefit, even if her earnings were small or nonexistent.

earner was much older than the spouse, this feature could create a major hardship.

Survivor's Benefits. The increasing frequency of two-earner couples has intensified a problem that arises after one spouse dies. Under current law, the surviving spouse receives a benefit based on the earnings record of the higher-earning spouse. In effect, the lesser-earning spouse's earnings record dies when either spouse dies. As a result, the survivor's benefit is no higher than it would have been if only the principal earner had worked. The survivor's benefit is one-third to one-half lower than what the couple received, although the poverty threshold is only one-fifth lower for a single elderly person than for an elderly couple.[10] This drop in benefits contributes to the fact that seven-eighths of aged couples had incomes above 150 percent of the 1999 poverty threshold, but only 58 percent of single elderly people living alone had income above the poverty threshold. In addition, some private pensions last only as long as the retired worker is alive, further reducing the income available to many surviving spouses.[11] Even if the pension continues for survivors, its value falls gradually because no private pension is fully adjusted for inflation.

Liberalizing the survivor benefit would improve the economic lot of survivors, a goal of increasing importance as life expectancy lengthens. Providing survivors with three-quarters of the couple's combined benefit would increase support for most widows and widowers. When combined with the previous proposal to reduce the spouse's benefit from one-half to one-third of the primary worker's pension, this initiative would ensure survivors a higher benefit than does the current system if their earnings entitled them to a benefit equal to at least one-third of their spouses' pensions. Most women retiring in the future would gain from this change because most will have long earnings histories. The added costs associated with this proposal would be almost completely offset by the savings achieved by reducing the spouse's benefit (see Table 6–1).

THE RETIREMENT AGE

Social Security has a profound effect on when people choose to retire. Two aspects of the program are of particular importance—the age at which retirement benefits are first available and the amount of benefits available at each age. Initially, Social Security retirement benefits were not available until age 65, and this age came to be known as "the retirement age." Then, in 1956, the program was liberalized for women, who became eligible for benefits at age 62. A similar change was made for men in 1961, and age 62 became "the age of initial entitlement."

Most workers began to claim benefits before age 65. But those who did so had to accept reduced pensions. Sixty-two-year-old claimants received 80 percent of what they would have been awarded at age 65, the "full-benefits" age.

In 1983, legislation was enacted that had the effect of lowering benefits. The 1983 legislation was cast as an increase in the full-benefits age, from age 65 to 67—or, in common parlance, as an "increase in the retirement age." In fact, the change did not alter the age of initial entitlement, and, as noted, most people claim benefits before age 65. Technically, the age at which full benefits will be paid is to be increased two months a year between 2000 and 2005 and then, after a twelve-year pause, again between 2017 and 2022. The full-benefits age will then be 67, meaning that workers retiring at age 67 will receive the same benefit that they would have received at age 65 under prior law.[12] At that point, age 62 retirees will receive 70 percent of the pensions they would be awarded if they claimed benefits at age 67.

If workers claim benefits after the full-benefits age, their pension is increased through the delayed retirement credit. At age 70, benefits are paid automatically. Table 6–2 (page 108) shows how benefits increase for workers turning age 62 in 2001 if they delay retirement up to age 70. Congress has steadily liberalized the delayed retirement credit. Starting in 2005 the increment will be 10 percent of benefits payable at age 62 for each year an individual works past the full-benefits age. At that time, the present value of the total benefits the average worker can be expected to receive during retirement will be independent of the age at which benefits are first claimed. That is, the higher benefits workers will receive for deferring claims after age 62 will just about offset the shortened expected duration of payments. Since all workers differ in some ways from the "average" worker, many are unsure when it is best to claim benefits (see Box 6–3, page 109).

Raising the Age of Initial Entitlement. Because Congress did not raise the age of *initial eligibility* in 1983 when it increased the full-benefits age, it set in motion changes that would lower the already meager benefits of early retirees, their spouses, and their survivors. A

Table 6–2
Benefits Payable to Workers Turning Age 62
in 2001, Depending on Age of Initial Benefit

If Benefit Is Claimed at Age. . .	Benefit as Percentage of What Is Payable at Age 62
62	100
63	108.3
64	116.5
65	124.8
66	133.6
67	142.6
68	151.5
69	160.4
70 or later	169.4

Source: Authors' calculations based on data from the Social Security Administration website, http://www.ssa.gov/OACT/ProgData/ar_drc.html.

modest increase in the age at which Social Security benefits first become available could encourage somewhat later retirement. It also would prevent people from agreeing to the large benefit reductions that come by claiming benefits early. We propose that the age of initial eligibility be increased from age 62 to age 64 over the same period that the age at which unreduced benefits are paid rises from 65 to 67. Such a change would assure more adequate retirement incomes for workers and their surviving spouses and would modestly lower program costs. It would also enlarge the labor force, boost national production, and reduce the burden of supporting the economically inactive.[13] This effect is significant because annual growth of the working age population over the next three decades is projected to be less than one-third the pace of the past thirty years.

Like any other restriction on benefits, an increase in the age of initial eligibility produces some losers. Many workers yearn to retire, as indicated by the fact that one-seventh of men still working at age 61 retire during the first year they become eligible for Social Security benefits and one-quarter are retired by age 63. Some people find work particularly onerous or dull. For others Social Security is the financial margin that permits long-awaited retirement. Although delaying initial claims would increase later retirement incomes, the delay in Social Security benefits would be a short-term loss for these groups. For still others—those with physical impairments or psychological problems—

Box 6–3
Should You Claim Benefits at
Age 62 or Wait until Later?

Should you claim Social Security benefits at the first opportunity, just after you turn age 62? Or should you wait until age 65 or even later?

Delaying your claim increases the benefits you receive for the rest of your life (see Table 6–2). If you are the primary earner, it also increases the benefits to which your spouse will be entitled should you die first. The increase is 8 1/3 percent for each year you delay *claiming* benefits from age 62 to the full benefits age even if you do not work past age 62. That means if you wait to age 65 to claim benefits, you will receive a 25 percent larger benefit for the rest of your life than you would receive if you claimed benefits at age 62. If you wait to claim benefits until age 70, payments will be 70 percent higher than they would be if claimed at age 62. Furthermore, if you work past age 62 and those earnings are among the highest thirty-five of your career, your benefits will increase even more.

The adjustments in benefits before age 65 were set in place about three decades ago to compensate the *average beneficiary* of that time for delay. Since life expectancies have increased, the average worker now lives longer and is more likely to benefit from claiming benefits later than he or she would have been in the past. The adjustment in benefits after the "full-benefits" age, which is 65 and 4 months for workers turning age 62 in 2001, is 7 percent and will rise to 8 percent for workers reaching age 62 after 2005.

What is true *on the average*, however, cannot be true for each person since personal circumstances differ greatly. For two groups, it makes financial sense to defer claiming benefits as long as possible. The first group consists of people who are healthy and come from families that have longer than average life expectancies. For this group, it generally makes sense to wait to claim benefits until age 65 or even later, if health and economic circumstances permit. A 25 percent benefit increase that just compensates the average beneficiary with average life expectancy will provide a windfall for people who can expect to live longer than average.

The second group consists of principal earners who are married to spouses considerably younger than they are, especially if the earner is male. The lesser-earning spouse can anticipate an extended period of widowhood—a woman who is married to a man eight years older than she is can expect to spend about eleven years as a widow. Waiting increases the benefit the widow (or widower) will receive.

In both cases, waiting may turn out to be a mistake for particular individuals, and each person must consider his or her personal circumstances. Even the daily jogger who is the offspring of centenarians may be struck down unexpectedly. The young widow may die prematurely. But the odds make waiting to claim benefits a good bet.

---

the delay in Social Security benefits can be a significant hardship. To protect this group, any increase in the age of initial eligibility for Social Security should be accompanied by relaxation of the test for disability insurance benefits for those age 62 to 64, which would reduce the savings shown in Table 6–1.

Raising the Full-Benefits Age. As life expectancy increases, the nation will have to decide whether pensions should continue to be available as early as age 62 and how much should be paid at each age. The greater the proportion of one's life spent in retirement, the greater the proportion of lifetime income that must be saved or the higher that taxes earmarked to support pensions must be if consumption is to be maintained after retirement.

Many Social Security reform plans would cut benefits by increasing the full-benefits age beyond 67, to 68, 70, or even later. The stated justification for additional increases is that life expectancy at age 65 has increased by more than four years since the program was enacted in 1935. Since these proposals do not call for any change in the age of initial eligibility, the linkage of life expectancy to the retirement age is misleading. They are simply benefit cuts.

Most people say that they oppose benefit cuts, which is not surprising considering that Social Security benefits are modest compared either to those of foreign nations or to our own poverty thresholds. Nonetheless, some benefit cuts will be necessary if revenue increases are not to bear the full burden of closing the projected long-term deficit. We propose that the benefit reduction enacted in 1983 be phased in without the twelve-year hiatus between 2005 and 2017. The cuts enacted in 1983 would be completed in 2011, not 2022. After 2011, we propose that benefits for workers who retire at any given age be cut gradually as life expectancy increases. Workers who spent the same proportion of their adult lives in retirement as those turning 62 in 2011 would receive the same replacement rates. In other words, if retirement represented one-fourth of adult life in 2011, a one-year increase in adult longevity would lead to the benefit cut associated with a nine-month increase in the age at which unreduced benefits are paid.[14] These changes would reduce the projected long-term deficit by 38 percent.

AVERAGING PERIOD

Benefits are now based on the thirty-five years of highest adjusted earnings. For people with long careers, counting more than thirty-five years of earnings would tighten the linkage between benefits and average career earnings. For those with few years of taxable earnings—disproportionately women who take time out from working for childrearing—lengthening the averaging period would mean counting additional years with zero earnings. Tying benefits as closely as possible to full average earnings is the best way to fulfill Social Security's goal of replacing lost earnings. For that reason, we propose to increase the averaging period from 35 to 38 years. Offsetting the disproportionate effect of this change on women would be the increase in survivor's benefits, which would be of particular benefit to women. Extending the averaging period would cut benefits for the average worker by 3 percent and reduce the projected long-term deficit by 13 percent. The case for counting more years becomes stronger as the age at which unreduced benefits are first paid and the age of initial entitlement are increased.[15]

Indexing Benefits

Before 1972, Congress typically boosted benefits in election years to offset the inflation-related erosion in the purchasing power of benefits. In 1972, Congress adopted a formula to adjust benefits automatically. For many years, the Consumer Price Index (CPI), which is used to adjust Social Security benefits, overstated inflation.[16] The Bureau of Labor Statistics (BLS) has changed the way it calculates the CPI and has additional plans to improve the accuracy of the CPI. These changes have lowered the growth of the CPI, and this slowdown has reduced the projected long-term deficit of Social Security.[17] Some additional improvements in the Consumer Price Index may be made that would further slow its growth, but the timing and size of these changes is unclear.

Mismeasuring the CPI has large financial consequences because the CPI is used to adjust not only Social Security benefits, but also other government benefit programs, such as Supplemental Security Income, Veterans Compensation and Pensions, and Civil Service and Military Retirement, and to adjust personal income tax exemptions, the standard deduction, and tax brackets. Congress should provide the BLS with budget resources and personnel sufficient to make corrections expeditiously. Because the stakes are high and the issues are technical, it should also establish an advisory committee of nonpartisan outside experts to monitor progress.

While everyone believes that the CPI should be as accurate as possible, some analysts and elected officials have proposed that benefits should not be fully adjusted for inflation. Former Senator Daniel Patrick Moynihan (Democrat of New York) proposed to adjust benefits one percentage point less than the measured CPI. Former Senators Bob Kerrey (Democrat of Nebraska) and Alan Simpson (Republican of Wyoming) proposed full inflation adjustments only for the 30 percent of beneficiaries receiving the lowest benefits. Recipients of larger benefits would receive the same dollar increase paid to beneficiaries at the thirtieth percentile.

Beyond improving the accuracy of the CPI, curtailing inflation adjustments is unjustified. Less than full adjustment for inflation would cause the purchasing power of all benefits to fall continuously the longer pensioners receive retirement, disability, or survivor payments. The Kerrey-Simpson proposal would deny full adjustments to people of modest means who receive relatively large Social Security benefits but have little other income. At the same time, it would give full inflation adjustments to beneficiaries who receive small Social Security checks but whose spouses have high incomes and to those who enjoy generous public pensions earned through long careers with one of the states or localities that remain outside of the Social Security system. Many long-term beneficiaries already face declining living standards as their other income sources become depleted. Social insurance should not make that problem worse, particularly considering the steady rise of real incomes among the economically active.

EXTENDING COVERAGE

State and local governments have never been required to participate in Social Security. Initially, legal experts doubted whether the federal government could constitutionally force their participation. Although most experts now believe such power exists, the federal government has not exercised it. About one-fourth of state and local government employees remain outside Social Security, primarily in California, Texas, and Ohio. Most are covered by pension plans that provide benefits similar to those offered under Social Security or defined-benefit private employer pension plans.[18]

Extending Social Security coverage to all state and local workers is desirable for several reasons. First, although most eventually

earn eligibility for Social Security through work in covered employment before, during, or after their service as state or local government employees or as the spouse of a covered worker, making
coverage universal would eliminate certain gaps in disability insurance coverage, extend survivor benefits to their spouses, and provide
more retirees inflation-proof pensions based on career earnings.
Second, state and local employees who are outside Social Security
avoid a responsibility shared by other workers. Part of the payroll
tax goes to pay current benefits because past taxes were used to pay
past benefits, not to build reserves. Covered workers bear this cost;
workers outside the system escape it. We can see no good reason
for differential treatment. In addition, Social Security provides extra
benefits for low earners; these extra benefits are financed by paying
relatively less generous benefits to high earners than would result
under a proportional benefit formula. State and local employees
have higher than average earnings. By remaining outside Social
Security state and local employees avoid this responsibility as well.
Bringing into Social Security all newly hired workers in states and
localities now outside the system would reduce the projected long-
term deficit by 11 percent.[19]

TAXATION OF BENEFITS

If the Treasury had ruled that Social Security benefits were
taxed like other contributory pensions, all of Social Security benefits would have been included in adjusted gross income, except for
the part of benefits that returned the workers' share of payroll taxes.
The principle—that income should be taxed once—is applied to private pensions. Applying the same principle strictly to Social Security
would be complex because the worker's payroll tax is included in
income subject to the personal income tax, but neither the employer's
tax nor the extra benefits above those funded by workers' taxes are
subject to personal income tax. The benefit formula, which favors
low earners, further complicates the calculation. In 1979, the
Advisory Council on Social Security reported that application of the
same rules used for contributory private pensions would cause at
least 85 percent of Social Security benefits to be included in adjusted
gross income, corresponding to the employer's tax and the benefit
payments that exceed the combined taxes of employer and employee.

More than half a century ago, the Internal Revenue Service quite incomprehensibly ruled that Social Security benefits were a gratuity that was wholly exempt from the income tax. The vast majority of policy experts came to regard this ruling as an aberration. But the Treasury Department refused to reverse itself without congressional action, which did not come until 1983. In that year, legislation directed that up to half of Social Security benefits should be included in income subject to tax, but only for individuals and couples with incomes over $25,000 and $32,000, respectively. In 1993, Congress raised the portion of benefits subject to income tax to 85 percent, but only to the extent that individual income exceeded $34,000 and couples' income exceeded $44,000. Even now, however, the tax system treats Social Security benefits more favorably than it does contributory private pensions.

Treating Social Security and contributory private pensions alike would close 22 percent of the projected long-term Social Security deficit if the exemptions of $25,000 for single filers and $32,000 for couples were repealed and 7 percent if they were retained.

While the income tax revenues generated by taxing all other income sources are regarded as general revenues, those attributable to taxing Social Security benefits are earmarked for the Social Security and Medicare trust funds. Social Security's share reached $10.2 billion in 2000 and would have been $21 billion if the tax rules for private pensions had been applied to Social Security and the income thresholds removed. This policy is really a backdoor way of funneling general revenues into support for Social Security. Given the history of restricting Social Security investments to low-yielding Treasury securities and the use of Social Security to provide relatively generous treatment of early generations of beneficiaries who had not worked under the system for much of their working lives, such a backdoor general revenue transfer to the trust funds is justified.

INVESTMENT OF RESERVES

From the beginning, Social Security's trustees were allowed to invest reserves only in securities guaranteed as to principal and interest by the federal government. Most trust fund holdings consist of special, nonmarketable Treasury securities. Such bonds pay the average interest rate of outstanding Treasury securities that mature in four or more years. These special issues can be sold back to the Treasury at par at any time—a feature not available on publicly held notes and bonds. In contrast, marketable bond prices fluctuate before they mature. The prohibition against trust fund investments in private stocks or bonds arose in part because Congress feared that the trust funds' managers might have to sell at a loss. Officials were also concerned that such sales could depress values of assets also held in private portfolios. An even more important consideration was the fear that political pressures might permit trust fund managers to interfere with private business decisions.

It is not surprising that policymakers legislating in the midst of the Great Depression viewed government securities as the only appropriate investment vehicle for workers' retirement funds. The stock market collapse and widespread corporate bond defaults were vivid memories. Federal Reserve Chairman Alan Greenspan echoed those fears in 1998 in declaring his opposition to authorizing the investment of any part of Social Security reserves in private securities. Prohibiting such investments solved this problem in the simplest possible way.

This limitation has become increasingly costly as the size of the Social Security trust funds has grown. Starting in 1977 Congress authorized the accumulation of significant reserves, a move to "partial reserve financing." Poor economic performance delayed reserve accumulation, but further legislation in 1983, together with improved economic performance, initiated the steady growth of reserves. At the end of 2000, reserves exceeded $1 trillion and they are projected to grow to more than $6 trillion by 2024. Measures adopted to close the projected long-run deficit in Social Security would produce much larger reserves.

The larger the reserve, the greater the loss from restricting investments to low-yielding special Treasury issues. Such restrictions deny Social Security beneficiaries the full returns that their saving and investment in a diversified portfolio generates. To the extent that the trust funds' reserve accumulation adds to national saving, it produces total returns for the nation equal to the average return on *private* investment, which runs about 6 to 7 percent more than the rate of inflation. However, investments in government securities are projected to earn only 3 percent more than inflation over the next seventy-five years. Forcing Social Security to invest only in low-yielding assets raises the payroll tax rate necessary to sustain any given level of benefits. Conversely, for any given tax rate, investment restrictions lower the benefits pensioners will receive. This penalty is particularly oner-ous for the majority of retirees who derive most of their incomes from Social Security.

The practical question is how best to avoid these disadvantages. Three ways exist. Each raises trust fund returns. Each brings to pen-sioners a larger share of the added economic returns that increased pension saving generates. But each has its own shortcomings. In chap-ter 5, we examined one in detail—privatization permits holders of personal retirement accounts to make diversified investments that may earn higher returns but could produce losses. Privatization forces individual workers to shoulder risks they are ill-equipped to bear, and under some variants, it also generates large and wasteful admin-istrative expenses.

Two other changes to the current system would bring workers the benefits of diversified investments while preserving the benefit secu-rity and low administrative costs of Social Security.

General Revenues. The simplest option would be to use general revenues to compensate the trust funds for the reduced yield resulting from investment restrictions. This approach had little appeal when the non-Social Security budget was in deficit. At that time, general rev-enue transfers would probably have led to yet larger deficits. The additions to the trust funds would have added nothing to national saving, investment, or economic growth. Now that the non–Social Security budget is in surplus and these surpluses are projected to con-tinue for years to come, the case for such transfers is strong. To the extent that general revenue transfers to Social Security reserves replace tax cuts or increased non-Social Security spending, they will boost saving, investment, and economic growth, thereby increasing the capacity of the nation to meet future pension obligations.

Three qualitative arguments support such general revenue trans-fers. First, congressional restrictions have denied Social Security ben-eficiaries the returns they could have enjoyed if reserves had been invested in a prudently diversified portfolio of government bonds and private stocks and bonds. Even if one believes such restrictions are necessary, workers covered by Social Security should not be denied the returns on accumulated Social Security reserves that they would have enjoyed if the funds had been privately managed, as the eco-nomic effects of Social Security reserve accumulation are identical to those of private pension reserve accumulation. If these restrictions had not applied, Social Security reserves would have been $1.6 trillion at the end of 1999 instead of the actual balance of $896 billion, a difference of $674 billion. A general revenue transfer of that amount would simply compensate covered workers for the economic cost of a restriction that elected officials deemed necessary because they were not convinced they could forbear meddling in private investment decisions. The transfer required to make up the shortfall in 1999 alone, when the trust funds' average balance was approximately $830 billion, would have been about $37 billion based on actual returns in 1999 on private stocks and bonds and $46 billion based on their long-term average rates of return. By comparison, the transfer of income taxes on benefits totaled $11.6 billion.

General revenue transfers are justified for a second reason—to pay for the unfunded liability of the Social Security system. Because future retirees and their employers will pay enough in taxes to buy the benefits they will ultimately receive, based on a modest rate of return, they are not the source of the projected long-term liability. The long-term deficit is approximated by the unfunded liability that results from the generous benefits paid to early pensioners, who received far more than their taxes could justify at a fair market rate of return. As noted in Box 6–4 (page 118), that unfunded liability is about $3 trillion over the next seventy-five years based on the assumption that Social Security benefits and taxes continue at legislated levels.

Finally, general revenue transfers are justified because Social Security performs functions that otherwise would fall to welfare programs for the elderly that are financed from general revenues, including Supplemental Security Income and its predecessor, Old Age Assistance. Computing exactly how much Social Security has reduced public assistance payments to the aged and disabled is a somewhat arbitrary exercise. But the fact that Social Security removes 39 percent of the elderly beneficiaries from poverty makes clear that Social Security is shouldering a burden that, in its absence, would be borne by the general taxpayer.

General revenue transfers to social insurance plans are commonplace around the world. They provide one-fifth or more of revenues for retirement pensions in Australia, Denmark, Germany, Japan, New Zealand, and Switzerland. Many early supporters proposed that one-third of Social Security revenue should come from general revenues, and some attacked the actual system because it relied exclusively on payroll taxes. In his fiscal 2000 and 2001 budgets, President Clinton

BOX 6–4
WHAT IS THE UNFUNDED LIABILITY?

The first workers who received Social Security benefits in 1940 had paid payroll taxes for at most three years. At a rate of 1 percent each on workers and their employers on earnings up to $3,000 a year, these taxes could not possibly have paid for the benefits that workers retiring at age 65 could expect to receive over their lifetimes. The same could be said for most workers who have claimed benefits since.

The difference between the value of payroll taxes collected from these retirees and the benefits actually paid to them came from the payroll taxes collected from still-active workers. These tax revenues did not accumulate to support the future benefits of the active workers. The gap between the accruing benefit obligations to still-active workers and Social Security reserves constitutes an "unfunded liability."

The concept of an unfunded liability is easy to describe but hard to measure. Its exact size depends on assumptions about future payroll tax collections and future accruals of benefit entitlements. Two alternative approaches illustrate the problem.

Under the first approach, Social Security is assumed to remain in existence with no change in law. Payroll taxes continue to be collected at currently legislated rates, and entitlements to future benefits continue to accrue. In short, Social Security remains open for business. Under these assumptions, the "open-group" unfunded liability is estimated to be $3 trillion in the year 2000. This sum is the present value of the long-term actuarial deficit, which is usually expressed as a percentage of covered taxable payroll. The unfunded liability is expressed in dollars.

Under the second approach, Social Security is projected to be terminated. No further payroll taxes are collected. No further benefit entitlements accrue. But workers who have already begun to contribute are assumed eventually to receive the benefits that they have earned to date–when they retire, are disabled, or become eligible for survivor benefits. Workers with fifteen years of earnings credits, for example, would be assumed to have accrued 15/35ths of the benefits they would eventually have earned had their earnings continued at the same level (earnings covering thirty-five years are averaged in computing lifetime benefits). The present value of this fraction of benefits they would have been expected to receive is the accrued liability. Under this so-called closed-group method, the unfunded liability of Social Security is about $11 trillion.

The "open-group" unfunded liability is equal to the lump-sum transfer that would restore exact financial balance to the current Social Security system for the duration of the projection period. General revenue transfers of that amount would result in the projected long-term balance. The "closed-group" unfunded liability is a measure of the cost of transition for the current Social Security system to a plan based entirely on individual accounts, under the assumption that all accrued benefits are paid when due.

proposed that general revenues be transferred to the trust fund in amounts equal to interest saving to the Treasury that have been realized because Social Security's surpluses have been used to pay down the national debt. These general revenue transfers, which would start in 2011 and continue for four decades, were projected to reduce the projected long-term deficit from 1.89 percent of payroll to 0.86 percent of payroll, a reduction of 54 percent.

Despite its simplicity and clear linkage to restrictions placed on the trust funds' investments and to the welfare-like transfers made to early beneficiaries, general revenue transfers provoke opposition.[20] Some argue that such transfers "paper over" the real long-term financing problem of Social Security. This criticism is not well founded if the alternative to transferring revenues to Social Security is either tax cuts or spending increases, both of which would raise current consumption. Others argue that general revenue financing would weaken the social insurance rationale through which payroll tax contributions create an "earned right" to benefits. Whether this weakening would occur is a matter of political judgment, and any such cost must be balanced against improved equity for workers.

For these reasons, we recommend that the federal government commit to a program of general revenue transfers to Social Security. The transfers, starting in 2002, would equal $100 billion or approximately 0.9 percent of GDP and would remain at that share of GDP. The transfers would continue until 2023, at which point the cumulative transfers would amount to about half of the currently projected long-term deficit.

Direct Investments in Private Securities. Some policymakers and analysts have concluded that part of the trust funds' reserves should be invested in private stocks and bonds. But these proposals have met criticism on both economic and political grounds. It is argued by some that merely shifting the trust funds' investments from government to private securities would not directly affect national saving, investment, the capital stock, or production. This objection is correct for *shifts in funds* from the current trust funds to private sector investments. But it ignores the fact that continued limits on trust fund investment deny workers the full economic returns from the added saving their payroll taxes represent. *Future additions* to the trust fund will raise saving and investment as well. The nation must decide whether workers and pensioners should continue to be denied credits for the economic benefits their saving produces.

The political question, which has troubled Congress since the inception of Social Security, concerns the possibility that the trust funds' investments in private securities might lead to inappropriate government influence over private companies. Private and state government pension funds sometimes vote their shares to change the policies of companies whose shares they own. The fear is that Social Security trustees might be subject to political pressures that force them to sell shares in companies making or selling products some people regard as noxious (for example, cigarettes or napalm) or that pursue business practices some people regard as objectionable (such as hiring children or paying very low wages in other countries, polluting, or not providing health insurance for their workers). Alternatively, the critics fear that the trust funds would retain shares in such companies and use stockholder voting power to try to exercise control over private companies.

A good deal of experience shows that these concerns are exaggerated, however. Several government trust funds now invest in private securities. Managers of the Thrift Savings Plan for government workers and the pension plans of the Federal Reserve Board, the U.S. Air Force, and the Tennessee Valley Authority have not exercised any control over the companies in which they invest and have pursued only financial objectives in selecting portfolios (see Box 6–5). This experience indicates that similar arrangements could also protect Social Security trustees from succumbing to political pressures. We describe institutions that would build upon this experience, but contain additional safeguards to protect investments of Social Security reserves in private securities.

The Federal Government as Creditor. The issue of the federal government holding private assets is becoming important for reasons independent of the handling of Social Security reserves. As of year end 2000, projected federal budget surpluses will be sufficient to buy back outstanding publicly held debt before 2010. Because the public may not offer all debt for sale, projections made during mid-2000 indicated that the federal government would begin to accumulate cash reserves starting in 2007. At that point, the Treasury will have to decide how to invest U.S. budget surpluses. It is important, therefore, to design

---

BOX 6–5
FEDERAL INVESTMENT IN PRIVATE SECURITIES

All federal employees hired since 1984 are covered by the Federal Employees Retirement System (FERS) and have the option of participating in the Thrift Savings Plan (TSP). TSP gives participants the option of contributing to five index funds: a government securities investment (G) fund, a common stock index investment (C) fund, a fixed income investment (F) fund, and, as of May 2001, a small-capitalization stock index (S) fund and an international stock index (I) fund.

The TSP had 2.5 million individual accounts at the end of August 2000. Assets totaled over $102 billion. Administrative costs varied from 8 to 10 basis points. Participants in FERS receive an automatic contribution to their TSP accounts from their employing agency equal to 1 percent of their basic pay. Employees can contribute up to 10 percent of their salary on a pretax basis. Their agencies match the first 3 percentage points of these contributions on a dollar-for-dollar basis and the next 2 percentage points on a $1-for-every-$2 basis.

The Federal Retirement Thrift Investment Board, which manages the three funds, consists of an executive director and five members appointed by the president. To minimize chances of political interference, the G fund is invested exclusively in short-term, nonmarketable special Treasury issues, the F fund is invested in an index mutual fund that tracks the Lehman Brothers Aggregate bond index, and the C fund in an equity mutual fund that tracks the Standard and Poor's 500 stock index. The C and F funds are managed under contract by the largest private manager of index funds in the United States.

Congress explicitly considered whether to model the TSP on individual retirement accounts, which permit account holders to select among a broad menu of private stocks and funds, but opted instead for centralized management. It stated its reasons in the *Congressional Record* (H.R. Rep. No. 99–606, pp. 137–38):

> As an alternative the committee considered permitting any qualified institution to offer [employees] specific investment vehicles. However, the committee rejected that approach for a number of reasons. First, there are literally thousands of qualified institutions who would bombard employees with promotions for their services. The committee concluded that employees would not favor such an approach. Second, few, if any, private employers offer such an arrangement. Third, even qualified institutions go bankrupt occasionally and a substantial portion of an employee's retirement benefit could be wiped out. This is in contrast to the diversified fund approach, which could easily survive a few bankruptcies. Fourth, it would be difficult to administer. Fifth, this "retail" or "voucher" approach would give up the economic advantage of this group's wholesale purchasing power derived from its large size, so that employees acting individually would get less for their money.

institutions that will permit government surpluses to be invested in ways that will neither disturb the operation of private financial markets nor permit government interference through financial transactions in the business decisions of private companies, *whether or not Social Security reserves are invested in private securities.*

The Fiduciary Corporation. Organizational reforms could all but eliminate the risk that Social Security reserves could be used to interfere with private investment decisions. Management of Social Security reserves could be placed in the hands of a private, not-for-profit entity created under federal charter—the Fiduciary Corporation (FC). The directors of the FC would consist of selected executives from the private sector and an independent government agency. Each would serve ex officio. For example, the federal charter might specify that the FC directors would include the president of one of the nation's largest insurance companies, the CEO of a major financial institution, the head of one of the leading stock exchanges, and the comptroller general from the General Accounting Office. The firms and exchanges from which the ex officio private sector members were drawn would rotate every five years among the largest three entities. The chair would be appointed under the rules used for governors of the Federal Reserve Board. That is, the president would nominate the chair, who would be confirmed by the Senate, to serve a fourteen-year term that could not be shortened for political reasons.

To manage the trust funds' reserves, the power of the FC would be statutorily limited to selecting fund managers on the basis of competitive bids. The fund managers would be authorized only to make passive investments in securities—bonds or stocks—of companies chosen to represent the broadest market indexes. These investments would have to be merged with funds managed on behalf of private account holders. To prevent the FC or its fund managers from exercising any voice in management of private companies and FC share ownership from diluting control of private shareholders, Congress could insist on either of two precautions. It could eliminate voting rights on shares held by the FC. Or it could employ a sufficient number of fund managers so that total shares voted by each manager would be less than a target proportion of outstanding stock of any company—say 1 percent. Under this option, fund managers would be required by law to vote shares solely in the economic interest of future beneficiaries.

This system would triply insulate fund management from political influence from elected officials. Trustees chosen from the private sector and serving ex officio and the presidentially appointed chair with a long-term appointment and security of tenure would protect the FC from political interference. Limitation of investments to passively managed funds and pooling with private accounts would prevent the FC from exercising power by selecting shares. The elimination or diffusion of voting rights among independent fund managers would prevent the FC from using voting power to influence company management. Furthermore, it would protect voting rights of private shareholders from dilution. Congress and the president would have no effective way to influence private companies through the trust funds unless they revamped the FC structure through legislation. While nothing other than a constitutional amendment can prevent Congress from repealing or modifying a previously enacted law, the political costs of doing so would be high. Furthermore, should Congress feel the urge to influence the policies of private businesses, it has many far more powerful and direct instruments to accomplish its ends than through management of the Social Security trust funds. The federal government can tax, regulate, or subsidize private companies to encourage or force them to engage in or desist from particular policies. No private company or lower level of government has similar powers.

It is important to note that private retirement accounts are not immune to political control. Congress could stipulate that savings in tax-sheltered accounts will not qualify for favored tax treatment if investments do not meet certain federally established requirements—such as directing a certain portion of funds to stipulated social objectives or avoiding investments in companies that engage in objectionable activities. Congress also could deny tax advantages to funds that act contrary to public policy. Such regulations would be politically viable only under extraordinary conditions, but these conditions would be no more extraordinary than those under which the procedural safeguards we have outlined for Social Security could be breached. With these institutional safeguards in place, we recommend that a portion of Social Security reserves be gradually invested in a broad mix of private securities.

How much such investment diversification would improve the financial prospects of Social Security would depend on the share of trust fund assets invested in private securities, especially common stocks, which over the long run have generated returns well in excess of yields on government or private bonds. In his 2000 budget and again in his 2001 budget, President Clinton proposed both to transfer general revenues to the trust funds and to authorize the Social Security trustees to hire private fund managers to invest gradually part of the trust funds in common stocks. The investments in private securities would have begun in 2010 and increased until 15 percent of the trust funds were invested in private securities in 2017. It was estimated that the investment of part of the reserves in private securities would reduce the projected long-term deficit by 0.20 percent of payroll. Congress did not act on this recommendation, and President Clinton subsequently withdrew it.

We believe that there is no good reason to deny covered workers and pensioners the benefits of returns from a prudently diversified portfolio. Institutions can be designed that would preclude use of such investments to interfere in the management of private businesses. Such institutions are likely to be needed in any event if federal budget surpluses continue. In particular, we recommend that upon formation of a Fiduciary Corporation the trust funds begin immediately to invest 1 percent of reserves a year in common stocks until holdings reach 20 percent of reserves but not more than 10 percent of total outstanding equities. We recommend also that the trust funds be authorized to invest in bonds of federal agencies that are not guaranteed as to principal and interest and in bonds of private corporations holding government-guaranteed mortgages such as those of the Federal National Mortgage Association until holdings equal half of the outstanding securities of such organizations. The added returns from both of these investment diversifications would reduce the projected long-term deficit of the Social Security system by 22 percent.[21]

Maintaining Funding

Under the economic and demographic assumptions now used to evaluate the long-run solvency of Social Security, the measures we have recommended are sufficient to generate large and growing Social Security surpluses, not just over the next seventy-five years but indefinitely. Of course, economic and demographic developments will not unfold precisely as current projections assume. Future adjustments in benefits or taxes will be necessary to maintain long-run balance. Policymakers have tended to procrastinate when the required adjustments involve imposing pain on beneficiaries or taxpayers. For this reason, an automatic adjustment mechanism should be part of a strengthened and modernized Social Security program. Specifically, Congress should enact legislation requiring it to consider, under expedited procedures, legislation to correct the imbalance if revenues and reserves fall 5 percent or more below expenditures projected over the next seventy-five years. If Congress failed to act within a set period—say, one year from notification—automatic tax increases and benefit cuts would take effect, each sufficient to close half of the projected deficit.

CONCLUSION

We have described changes in Social Security sufficient to convert the projected long-term deficit into a projected surplus (see Table 6–1). Most of the changes in benefits are cuts, but we also propose increased benefits for widows and widowers. Although our menu includes an increase in the portion of benefits subject to tax, no tax increase is needed to restore long-term balance. The menu includes sizable general revenue transfers so that the burden of paying off the unfunded liability does not fall exclusively on workers in proportion to their earnings. It calls for the creation of a government-chartered, private corporation to hire fund managers to manage investment of approximately one-fifth of trust fund reserves in common stocks and a larger share in bonds and notes that are not guaranteed as to interest and principal by the federal government.

Most important, the menu closes the projected long-term deficit with room to spare. It does so without modifying the basic structure and key strengths of the current Social Security system—the defined-benefit pension structure, which protects workers from financial market and other risks to their safety-net income; the social assistance to low earners, strengthened by improved protection of widows and widowers; and full adjustment for correctly measured inflation.

These reforms would also build and maintain an enlarged trust fund. This fund would raise national saving, provided that future Congresses and presidents do not use the program's surpluses to mask deficits in the other operations of government or to justify benefit increases or tax cuts in Social Security.

The budget history of the past decade gives some reason for optimism. As Social Security reserves have risen from less than three months of benefit payments in 1985 to thirty months of benefit payments at the end of 2000, Congress has eliminated large and growing deficits on other operations of government and created a vista of ever increasing surpluses. The growth of Social Security reserves did not derail the deficit reduction programs enacted in 1990, 1993, and 1997. This legislation, along with economic growth, turned a deficit on operations of government other than Social Security of 5.4 percent of GDP in 1985 into a surplus of 0.9 percent of GDP in 2000.

The real test, however, has just begun. Blessed by the kind of budgetary elbow room that elected officials have not experienced in decades, the president and Congress will be tempted to use budget surpluses to fund tax cuts and spending increases. Both would lead to increased consumption, private or public. While increased current consumption is tempting, the nation faces heavy obligations to provide pension and health benefits to the retiring baby boomers. Now is the time to prepare to meet those costs—by saving more, not by consuming more. In this environment, a policy of transferring some of the surpluses in the non-Social Security budget to Social Security would boost national saving.

If Social Security's long-run financial balance is restored and part of reserves is invested in private securities, as we urge, it will be important to make sure that good news surprises do not lead to unwise benefit expansions. For example, should asset prices rise faster than assumed in the actuarial projections, Social Security might appear to be overfunded. Such a windfall might tempt elected officials to enact politically popular benefit increases or tax cuts. Should asset prices subsequently decline, we fear that elected officials would be loath to cut benefits or raise taxes.

We propose that Congress enact targets for trust fund accumulation similar in general structure to those it has established for private defined-benefit pension funds under the Employee Retirement Income Security Act. Furthermore, the Fiduciary Corporation should be required to evaluate all proposed changes to Social Security benefits and taxes to determine if the legislation would retard achievement of these targets. If the FC judged that the proposed legislation would reduce the trust funds' balance over a five-, ten-, or seventy-five-year period, a supermajority vote would be required for Senate passage.[22] In the House of Representatives, no similar restraint is possible because a majority vote determines the rules under which each piece of legislation is considered. Even in the House, however, a negative report from the FC would inhibit legislation that would jeopardize the financial soundness of Social Security.

In addition, the operations of Social Security, which are now officially "off-budget," should be removed from the main budget totals reported by the Office of Management and Budget and the Congressional Budget Office. Budget resolutions enacted annually to guide congressional action should exclude Social Security from aggregate totals.

7

PROPOSALS TO REFORM SOCIAL SECURITY: A REPORT CARD

Policymakers and the public face a lengthy and bewildering menu of proposals to reform or replace Social Security. Think tank scholars have generated numerous plans. The 1994–96 Advisory Council on Social Security crafted three different proposals. Two called for the introduction of private accounts, one for strengthening the current system. None received majority support. More than a dozen different proposals, sponsored or cosponsored by more than seventy-five members, were introduced in the 106th Congress. Some of these plans called for full privatization of Social Security, some called for partial privatization, and others sought to restore balance in the current system. President Clinton proposed a plan to strengthen the financial underpinnings of the current Social Security system. He also advocated a new program of retirement savings accounts funded by individual contributions matched progressively with tax credits. Then the two major-party candidates during the hard-fought 2000 presidential campaign presented sharply different visions for how Social Security should evolve.

Fortunately for the interested citizen, all of the proposals receiving serious attention fall into one of three categories: plans to strengthen and modernize the current system, plans to replace the current system entirely with private accounts, and plans to transform the current system into a hybrid consisting of a scaled-back Social Security program supplemented by private accounts. The distinction between partial and complete privatization is somewhat fuzzy because it takes many years to transform a large, complex program like Social Security that is vital to the well-being of millions of vulnerable Americans. All full privatization plans phase in over several decades. During that transition, Social Security would continue to provide pensions to all current retirees and workers above stipulated ages and would govern, in part, the pensions for all but the youngest workers. Some partial privatization plans are intended to be way stations toward a fully privatized system. For example, during his campaign for president George W. Bush advocated a proposal to privatize Social Security "partially." But he also suggested that the ultimate goal was something much more far-reaching when he declared that the government could not go "from one regime to another overnight. . . . It's going to take a while to transition to a system where personal savings accounts are the predominant part of the investment vehicle. And so, this is a step toward a completely different world and an important step."[1]

There are two other approaches to Social Security reform—making retirement saving strictly voluntary and imposing means or income tests as a condition for receiving benefits. For the reasons we describe in Boxes 3–6 and 7–1, we think these approaches are both ill considered and unworkable.

In this chapter, we examine six reform plans that reflect the range of approaches under active discussion. We evaluate these plans using four criteria to grade them from A to D.[2] No plan described here receives an overall failing grade of F because all would move toward restoring financial balance to the nation's basic retirement system. A grade of D means that we regard a plan as so severely flawed that it does not merit serious consideration. A grade of C means that a plan contains major shortcomings based on the criteria we propose. A grade of B means that a plan has significant strengths and meets most requirements for reform, but comes up short in one or more key respects. The grade of A means that a plan meets all major requirements for reform and falls seriously short in none. Not everyone will agree with our evaluations. Some may object to the particular criteria we have selected or the importance we attach to them. Others may think we have been too harsh or lenient in grading a particular plan. In the end, you must form your own judgment.

BOX 7–1
WHY MEANS TESTING OF SOCIAL
SECURITY DOES NOT MAKE SENSE

Peter G. Peterson, former secretary of commerce, has proposed that all federal benefits to individuals, including Social Security and Medicare, be subject to an affluence test.[a] Under this plan, which has been endorsed by the Concord Coalition, households with incomes at least $5,000 above the national median would have their benefits scaled back 1 percent for each $1,000 by which their annual income including benefits exceeded the threshold. In other words, a household with an income $30,000 above the threshold would have its benefits scaled back 30 percent. The maximum amount by which benefits could be reduced would be 85 percent.

This approach seeks to lower benefits most for those who need them least. This same principle is reflected in the current Social Security benefit formula, which provides higher replacement rates for workers with low average earnings than for workers with high average earnings. It also is the logic behind the progressive income tax.

Unfortunately, this principle would have undesirable consequences if applied to Social Security benefits. It would increase penalties on work and saving, raise insurmountable administrative problems, and undermine the basic rationale of Social Security.

To see how the affluence test would work if applied to income—and the problems it would generate—consider a retired wife receiving $10,000 a year in Social Security and her working husband who earns $30,000 a year. They also receive $25,000 in income from their investments. Given median income of $41,000 in 1999, the affluence test would reduce the retiree's Social Security by $1,900. If the retiree's husband stopped working, she would not suffer this benefit reduction. They also could avoid the affluence test in whole or in part if they shifted their investments into assets that generated little income but promised subsequent capital gains.

These responses, which would undermine the intent of an income test, could be minimized if the test were applied to net worth rather than annual income. Unfortunately, net worth tests are even more costly to administer than income tests, as they require annual valuations of all assets, many of which are not generally traded. Furthermore, asset tests are easily evaded now that the financial market is global.

An income test violates the fundamental political compact that underlies Social Security— that a lifetime of work in jobs requiring payment of the payroll tax entitles a worker to a benefit based on average earnings when that worker reaches retirement age. Without this principle, there would be no rationale for financing benefits with a payroll tax or relating benefits to past earnings. An income test upsets this principle by denying benefits, regardless of earnings or payroll taxes paid, to people who saved a lot, had earnings, were lucky in investments, or were blessed by significant inheritance. The principle of relating benefits to past earnings is not sacrosanct. But introducing an income or asset test would erode the political basis for payroll tax-supported social insurance.

---

a. Peter G. Peterson, *Will America Grow Up before It Grows Old?* (New York: Random House, 1996), and *Facing Up: How to Rescue the Economy from Crushing Debt and Restore the American Dream* (New York: Simon and Schuster, 1993).

CRITERIA FOR REFORM

Our first criterion requires that a good reform plan *ensure* benefits that are *adequate* and *equitably* distributed and represent a *fair return* for taxes paid. Complete guarantee of benefits is impossible under any approach. Congress has legal power to curtail public pensions, but it operates under severe political constraints and has never cut benefits for pensioners as a group by more than a few percent. Private asset markets, in contrast, have no such constraints. Assets may depreciate, and private financial organizations may go bankrupt.

Current benefits are not unduly generous, as we showed in Box 6–1. For that reason, *adequacy* means that large benefit cuts are unacceptable. They would result in insufficient support for retirees, the disabled, and survivors. Overall benefit increases also are undesirable because they would further swell the added costs future workers will bear to finance their own pensions as well as pay down the unfunded liability generated by past Social Security commitments. *Equity* requires that protection be maintained for low earners, large families, and other vulnerable people. And a *fair return* means that taxes or account contributions that go into reserves should be invested wisely and that plans should not incur needless administrative costs.

Our second criterion is that the unavoidable *risks of long-term pension commitments should be shared broadly*, not placed on the shoulders of individual workers. Our third criterion for judging plans *is administrative efficiency and feasibility*. In addition to avoiding needless administrative costs, the plan should not be unduly complex for private businesses, workers, and the government. Finally, we give higher grades to plans that *raise national saving*. A plan's contribution to national saving is determined by its additions to reserves held in either the trust funds or individual accounts, less any induced reductions in private saving outside the retirement system and any induced increase in public borrowing or reduced surpluses in the non–Social Security budget.

Other consequences of Social Security reform are important as well. How reform will influence retirement decisions, for example, will be of increasing importance because labor force growth will slow to a crawl during the first decades of the twenty-first century. Reform may also change the relative treatment of one- and two-earner couples, a subject of particular concern to the growing number of working women. While these—and many other—dimensions of reform are of concern, no plan should merit serious consideration if it provides in-adequate benefits, fails to protect low earners, and gives a poor return for each dollar of taxes paid; if it subjects workers to excessive risk; if it generates needless administrative complexity; and if it does nothing to boost national saving.

PROPOSALS TO REPLACE SOCIAL SECURITY

Several plans would replace Social Security in whole or in part with personal retirement accounts. The plans differ in how much assis-tance they would give low earners beyond the accumulation in each worker's personal account, how much discretion individuals would have to select investments for their accounts, how much control par-ticipants would have over the way benefits are paid from their per-sonal accounts when they retire, how much risk individual workers would face, how the plans would be administered, and how the costs of transition to the new system would be paid for.

THE ARCHER-SHAW PLAN

The Archer-Shaw plan—developed by Representative Bill Archer (Republican of Texas), chairman of the Committee on Ways and Means in the 106th Congress, and Representative E. Clay Shaw (Republican of Florida), chairman of that committee's Social Security Subcommittee—is an "add-on, partial-privatization" plan. "Add-on" means that the funds to finance private accounts come from revenues in addition to those from the current payroll tax. In this plan, the funds come from general revenues, which would pay for a refundable tax credit equal to 2 percent of a worker's wage subject to the Social Security payroll tax. Each year, this credit would be deposited direct-ly into a worker's private retirement account held in a qualified mutu-al fund supervised by a Social Security Guarantee Board. To qualify, a mutual fund must invest 60 percent of its assets in a common stock index fund and 40 percent in a representative mix of corporate bonds. Each year, the earnings on these investments, less 25 basis points (one-quarter of a percent of total asset value) for administrative expenses, would be credited to the worker's account. The govern-

TABLE 7–1
POLICIES TO REFORM SOCIAL SECURITY AND REDUCE THE LONG-TERM DEFICIT CONTAINED IN FOUR SOCIAL SECURITY REFORM PLANS

	Archer-Shaw	Gramm-Domenici	Breaux-Gregg	Social Security Modernization
Benefit Reductions				
1. Accelerate to 2011 the scheduled increase to 67 in age at which unreduced benefits are available			X	X
2. Increase age at which unreduced benefits are available to 70 by 2029			X	
3. After 1 or 2 above, increase age at which unreduced benefits are available to keep the fraction of adult life in retirement constant (*by one month every year and a half)			X*	X
4. Increase age of initial eligibility along with age at which unreduced benefits are available			X	X
5. Reduce spouse's benefit to one-third of worker's benefit			X	X
6. Average earnings over thirty-eight (*forty) years rather than thirty-five years when computing benefits			X*	X
7. Reduce replacement rate for those with higher average earnings			X	
8. Reduce disability benefits			X	
9. Reduce annual cost-of-living adjustment			X	

Proposal				
Benefit Increases				
10. Raise benefits for surviving spouse to 75 percent of the couple's combined benefit	X			
11. Ease disability requirements for those affected by the increase in the age of initial benefit eligibility	X			
Revenue Increases				
12. Subject more of benefits to the income tax	X			
13. Transfer general revenues to trust fund	X			
14. Invest the trust funds' reserves in private as well as government assets	X			
Individual Accounts				
15. Establish individual retirement accounts (*voluntary for current workers)		X		X
16. Individual accounts can be left to heirs if worker dies before retirement (*only if worker has no dependent or survivor beneficiaries)		X*	X	X*
17. Channel general revenues into private retirement accounts		X		X
Other				
18. Require all new state and local employees to join Social Security	X	X		X
19. Special minimum based on years of service		X		X

ment would use general revenues to reimburse fund managers for administrative expenses that exceeded 25 basis points.

When a worker reaches retirement age and claims benefits, the ownership of the funds in the personal account, which would remain invested 60 percent in stocks and 40 percent in bonds, would be transferred to the Social Security trust fund. The Social Security system would compute the value of the inflation-indexed annuity that these funds could support. If this annuity was smaller than the Social Security benefit that the worker would receive under the existing benefit formula, the worker would be given a Social Security benefit based upon his or her earnings history. If the individual account annuity was larger, the worker would receive that amount. The Social Security actuary estimates that, if the average yield on stocks and bonds and the variation around that average yield matches past performance, about 5 percent of funds accumulated in personal accounts would end up as additions to current-law Social Security benefits.[3]

The account balances of workers who die before becoming eligible for benefits would be transferred into the account of a surviving spouse. The balance of the individual accounts of deceased workers who have no relatives who qualify or will qualify for dependent or survivor's benefits would become part of the worker's estate, which would be transferred to heirs. In all other cases, balances in individual accounts would flow entirely to the Social Security fund to support survivor's and dependent benefits.

The Archer-Shaw plan relies on a significant infusion of general revenues, which it uses to build reserves in individual accounts. These new reserves generate increased returns because they are invested in a diversified portfolio of private securities. When the balances are transferred to the trust fund, they help to restore balance to the Social Security system. Eventually, these transfers are projected to grow so large that payroll taxes can be cut. The plan calls for a 2.5 percentage point payroll tax cut after fifty years and an additional 1 percentage point reduction ten years later. While payroll taxes will be lower under the plan, income taxes will be higher than otherwise would be necessary to sustain any level of non-Social Security spending without incurring a deficit in the non–Social Security budget accounts.

Benefit Adequacy and Equity. The Archer-Shaw plan gets a high mark for benefit adequacy, primarily because it maintains Social Security benefits. The plan deserves a somewhat lower grade for equity. The distribution of the extra benefits from individual accounts would tend to be inequitable and somewhat irrational. Almost all of the gain would flow to high earners and almost none to moderate and low earners. The reason is that the Social Security benefit formula is progressive; that is, on average high earners receive smaller benefits per dollar contributed in payroll taxes than do moderate and low earners. Individual account balances and the resultant annuities, in contrast, would be proportional to contributions. For that reason, only high earners, particularly single workers with high lifetime earnings, would be likely to receive pensions that exceeded those guaranteed by Social Security. This inequity would be ameliorated if payroll taxes, which are a significant burden to low-wage workers, were lowered as the Archer-Shaw plan envisions and the contributions to the individual accounts continued to be financed from general revenues, which are paid disproportionately by those with high incomes.

Protection against Risk. The plan exposes the vast majority of workers to little risk because they stand to receive nothing or very little from their individual accounts. For them, the risks associated with market fluctuations in asset prices are borne by the Social Security trust fund, which is extremely well suited to bear such uncertainties because it spreads risk among workers and over time. Those who will receive pensions based on the value of their individual accounts at retirement face only upside opportunity.

However, the political sustainability of the Archer-Shaw plan is uncertain. Individuals would participate in an elaborate system that would inform them periodically of deposits made into their individual accounts, accumulations in these accounts, and the future benefits that would result from these accumulations. In the end, however, few who lived to claim benefits from the system would actually get anything at all from their individual accounts; rather they would get the benefit guaranteed by Social Security. Such a system could breed cynicism and disillusionment. It is unlikely that workers would be content to watch their accounts build and then discover that there was nothing in them when they retired. For this reason, the plan's apparent protection of pensioners from risk could prove to be somewhat illusory.

Administrative Efficiency. In effect, the Archer-Shaw plan is an elaborate, indirect, and costly device for investing part of the government's budget surplus in private securities and capturing the higher assumed yields on these assets to remedy the imbalance in the Social Security trust fund. The plan would generate considerably higher administrative costs than would either the current system or a plan that transferred general revenues to the trust fund and required that these amounts be invested collectively in private assets. Not only would there be managerial costs for the qualified mutual funds and the millions of individual accounts, but the Social Security Administration also would face increased expenses monitoring the qualified funds, dealing with the accounts of deceased workers, and calculating and distributing the supplementary pensions.

Unlike many plans, the Archer-Shaw proposal has several design features that would limit administrative costs. Fund managers would be limited to investments in passively managed index funds. Deposits would be made only once a year. Workers would be permitted to shift their balances between funds at most annually. And each worker's account would have to be held by a single fund. Nevertheless, total administrative costs could exceed the 0.25 percent that could be charged against the investment yield on individual accounts.

The issue of costs is of great importance because the administrative expenses would apply to all funds on deposit, while only one dollar in twenty of these balances would actually represent increased benefits. If total administrative charges were 25 basis points (0.25 percent of funds on deposit per year), the cost over a forty-year period would equal approximately 5 percent of funds on deposit. If the average additional benefit represented only 5 percent of funds, costs would equal the total increase in benefits.

The trade-off is somewhat less unattractive if one compares administrative costs with a possible benefit reduction (or tax increase) that the Archer-Shaw plan would avoid. To balance the Social Security system over seventy-five years based on the actuarial projections released in 2000 would require a benefit cut of 12 percent averaged over the period. The Archer-Shaw plan would avoid this cut, but at the price of an increase in administrative costs of 5 percent of benefits. As we indicated in Chapter 6, there is a far less costly way of securing for Social Security the benefits of the increased yields on investments in a diversified portfolio of private securities.

National Saving. The Archer-Shaw plan would add to national saving to the extent that the refundable tax credit is financed out of non–Social Security budget surpluses that would otherwise be used to support tax cuts or spending increases. If the tax credits are financed by increased non–Social Security budget deficits or by surpluses that would otherwise be used to pay down debt, the plan has no direct effect on national saving. If the non-Social Security budget remains in surplus, diverting a portion of that surplus to building up pension reserves is likely to add to national saving. (See Table 7–2.)

TABLE 7–2
REPORT CARD FOR THE
ARCHER-SHAW SOCIAL SECURITY GUARANTEE PLAN

CRITERIA	GRADE
Adequacy, equity, and a fair return	B+
Protection against risk	B
Administrative efficiency	C
Increased national saving	A–
Overall grade	B

THE GRAMM-DOMENICI PLAN

Senators Phil Gramm (Republican of Texas) and Pete Domenici (Republican of New Mexico), two members who have been active in the effort to restructure Social Security, released a prospectus for a Social Security reform plan in 1998, but they have not translated this prospectus into legislative language. In November 2000, Senator Gramm published a description of the plan under his own name.[4] Under the plan as described by Senator Gramm, Social Security would gradually be transformed into a benefit guarantee that would back-stop pensions financed primarily from individual accounts. Initially, 3.1 percentage points of the payroll tax (5.1 percent for workers aged 35 to 55 in 2001) would be diverted from the Social Security trust fund to newly created individual accounts. These accounts would be managed by competing private investment companies.

Workers would receive a pension based on their individual account accumulation. But they would be guaranteed a total benefit at least equal to the Social Security benefit promised under current law. In the early years, before individual account balances built up, the Social Security guarantee would account for most of the benefits paid. Simulations released by Senator Gramm indicate that Social Security outlays would decline steadily as the individual accounts increased in size. By 2054, pensioners with average earnings would receive a benefit that Senator Gramm asserts would be about twice that promised under current law. This promise rests on the assumption that the individual accounts are invested 60 percent in stocks and 40 percent in corporate bonds, that those assets continue to earn their historical average rates of return of 5.5 percentage points more than inflation, and that a major increase in national saving attributed to the creation of individual accounts generates a large increase in corporate income tax collections, most of which is earmarked to support retirement pensions. Although returns could vary widely from cohort to cohort and from worker to worker, depending on market performance of their portfolios, retirees would be guaranteed pensions at least as large as those promised under current law.

As the proportion of the guaranteed pension derived from Social Security fell, an increasing share of the payroll tax would be shifted from Social Security to individual accounts. Eventually, payroll tax deposits in individual retirement accounts would rise from 3.1 percentage points to 8 percentage points of income. An additional 2 percentage points of payroll tax would be used to buy private disability insurance. Thus, the payroll tax would fall from 12.4 percent of earnings to 10 percent. Social Security would all but vanish, leaving only a benefit formula to serve as a measure of the minimum guarantee for each worker. Surviving spouses would continue to receive the same benefits as provided under current law until the payroll tax diverted to individual accounts reached 5 percentage points of income. At that point, the retirement annuity purchased for the worker would include family and survivor benefits. In these cases as well, current-law Social Security benefits would continue as a guaranteed minimum. If the worker died before retirement, accumulated balances less the value of survivor benefits would be paid as a tax-free lump sum to the family.

Because the plan would both continue to pay retirement benefits as large as or larger than those promised under current law and finance deposits into individual accounts, it would require more revenue than does the current system. During the early years, the major source would be borrowed general revenue. In addition, assumed increases in corporation income taxes would be earmarked to supplement payroll tax collections. This revenue would come from added investments that Senator Gramm assumes would result from the plan. He estimates that corporate tax transfers would rise steadily, exceeding $1 trillion a year by 2044 and $4 trillion a year by 2075. Accumulated Social Security reserves also would be used to finance benefits. Over time, the assumed higher rates of return on individual accounts would generate a surplus that could be used to pay off the initial borrowing and to lower payroll tax rates as well.

Benefit Adequacy and Equity. The Gramm-Domenici plan's benefits would be adequate—too adequate in our judgment. Given the large economic transfers to the baby-boom generation implicit in current benefit levels—including not only pensions but also the costs of Medicare Hospital Insurance and Supplemental Medical Insurance and Medicaid acute and long-term care benefits—it would be imprudent to commit now to increase pensions.

Furthermore, the added benefits from individual accounts will flow disproportionately to high earners for the same reasons laid out in the criticism of the Archer-Shaw plan. Because the Gramm-Domenici plan gives workers more flexibility with respect to investment choices, the disparity will be exacerbated by the tendency of high earners to accept more investment risk to capture higher returns.

Protection against Risk. If the plan works as assumed, workers would be ensured benefits at least as large as those provided by current law. But pensions would fluctuate with the price of assets underlying their variable annuity and with inflation. If overall returns are not as high as assumed, then the benefit guarantees could put severe fiscal pressures on the federal government. For reasons we explain below, the increases in corporate tax revenues on which the financing of the Gramm-Domenici plan depends are not likely to be realized. Cutting off that source of revenue would jeopardize the plan as a whole and place the entire benefit structure in considerable danger. Despite the claim that benefits would at least equal current Social Security benefits and would eventually greatly exceed them, we rank the Gramm-Domenici plan low because of its risky financing.

Administrative Efficiency. The Gramm-Domenici plan would generate more sizable administrative costs than the Archer-Shaw proposal. Having competing private financial companies would entail duplicative management structures. They would be under pressure to advertise and incur other marketing costs. They would be tempted to engage in wasteful trading in order to generate better than average investment records. In fact, the Gramm-Domenici plan's description of private accounts resembles arrangements in Latin America and Great Britain where administrative costs typically eat up 10 to 20 percent or more of the potential pension accumulation. The Gramm-Domenici plan, therefore, ranks low on administrative efficiency.

National Saving. The most serious problems with the Gramm-Domenici plan involve its financing. Revenues from added corporation income tax collections, it is claimed, would grow steadily and would come to account for an ever larger portion of revenues for the pension system. But there is no reason to expect that the Gramm-Domenici plan will actually boost saving, capital formation, or corporate profits in the near term. The Gramm-Domenici plan raises no taxes and cuts no pensions. Therefore, there is no mechanism through which it could increase saving. In fact, the promise of higher pensions may induce workers to save less privately for their retirement, lowering national saving.

Without an increase in saving, there is no basis for additional capital formation, in the corporate sector or elsewhere. The designers of this plan err by assuming that a dollar deposited in a private account adds more to saving than does a dollar added to Social Security reserves; it does not. The Gramm-Domenici plan promises a massive benefit increase but does not have the financial base to make good on those promises. On its effects on national saving, the Gramm-Domenici plan merits an F. (See Table 7–3.)

BREAUX-GREGG PLAN

The plan proposed by Senators John Breaux (Democrat of Louisiana), Judd Gregg (Republican of New Hampshire), and others would divert 2 percentage points of the current payroll tax to individual accounts modeled on the federal employees' Thrift Savings

TABLE 7–3
REPORT CARD FOR THE
GRAMM-DOMENICI SOCIAL SECURITY PRESERVATION PLAN

CRITERIA	GRADE
Adequacy, equity, and a fair return	B+
Protection against risk	C–
Administrative efficiency	D
Increased national saving	F
Overall grade	C–

Plan and cut Social Security benefits an average of 25 to 30 percent (see the appendix to this chapter and Table 7–1 for details).[5] Cuts of this size would be necessary both to close the current projected long-term deficit and to free up 2 percentage points of the payroll tax for individual savings accounts. Retiring workers would be required to convert a portion of their account balances into an inflation-protected annuity. Together with the retiree's reduced Social Security benefit, this annuity would have to be sufficient to meet a standard for minimum retirement income.

Social Security benefits would be cut in four ways: by increasing when unreduced benefits are available to age 70 by 2029 and at a slower pace thereafter, by reducing the spouse's benefit, by shaving the cost-of-living adjustment, and by cutting replacement rates for all retirees except those with average earnings below approximately $6,400 in 2000, a threshold that would rise at the same rate as average earnings. A new minimum benefit would be established that was equal to 60 percent of the poverty threshold for those with twenty years of covered earnings, rising to 100 percent of the poverty threshold for those with forty years of earnings. A fail-safe mechanism would automatically keep the program in long-run balance and ensure that the financial balance would not be jeopardized by unexpected developments.

Benefit Adequacy and Equity. The Breaux-Gregg plan combines mandatory individual accounts, administered along the lines of the Thrift Savings Plan, with a scaled-back Social Security system. It lowers both retirement and disability benefits significantly—30 to 40 percent for moderate and high earners. Cuts of this size are necessary because the plan widens the program's deficit by diverting payroll taxes from Social Security. As a consequence of these cuts, the guaranteed element of pension protection would be drastically curtailed. For that reason, we give the plan a low grade on this dimension.

Protection against Risk. Investment options and management of individual accounts would be patterned after those of the Thrift Savings Plan. Workers would be exposed to the risks of general market fluctuations in asset values (see Figure 3–1), but would not face the greater dangers associated with selecting individual stocks or riskier financial instruments. The requirement that a portion of the personal accounts be converted upon retirement into an inflation-indexed annuity would protect people from outliving some pensions or having all of their pensions eroded unduly by inflation. The minimum Social Security benefit, which would be set equal to the poverty threshold for a worker with forty years of participation, would provide, at least initially, considerable protection to low earners and those with low returns from their individual accounts. This safety net, however, would be less meaningful over time because real incomes would be pushed up by productivity growth, while the poverty threshold is adjusted only for inflation.

The minimum benefit could undermine political support for the system because it would weaken the fundamental relationship between earnings and contributions on the one hand and benefits on the other. Many moderate earners might end up receiving pensions based on the guaranteed minimum and wonder why they were paying more in payroll tax than low earners but getting nothing for it.

Administrative Efficiency. The central administration and investment management of the personal accounts, investment in a restricted number of index funds, and mandatory annuitization would hold down overhead costs of the Breaux-Gregg plan. The need to calculate the portion of each personal account that would have to be annuitized and the difficulties associated with administering both the annuity and the remaining balance would introduce some complexity.

National Saving. The Breaux-Gregg plan would boost national saving by dramatically lowering Social Security benefits, converting a projected long-term deficit into approximate balance. At the same time, the payroll taxes diverted from Social Security would go into individual accounts that would build sizable reserves. Overall, we give the Breaux-Gregg plan a grade of C+. (See Table 7–4.)

TABLE 7–4
REPORT CARD FOR THE
BREAUX-GREGG TWENTY-FIRST CENTURY RETIREMENT PLAN

Criteria	Grade
Adequacy, equity, and a fair return	C
Protection against risk	C
Administrative efficiency	C+
Increased national saving	B
Overall grade	C+

THE BUSH PRINCIPLES[6]

During his presidential campaign, George W. Bush endorsed an approach to Social Security reform that would give workers the option of transferring part of their payroll taxes into individual accounts. He confined his statements to broad principles, however, and announced no specific plan. The details, he said, would be fleshed out by a bipartisan commission he promised to appoint when he took office. The principles Bush endorsed were that:

◆ Social Security should not be changed for retirees or for workers near retirement;

◆ payroll taxes should not be increased;

◆ the Trust Fund reserves should not be invested in common stocks;

◆   disability and survivor's benefits should not be changed;

◆   workers should be permitted, but not required, to shift a portion
     of their payroll taxes from the Social Security trust funds into
     individual accounts; and

◆   Social Security's surpluses should not be used to finance other
     government spending or tax cuts.

Presumably, Social Security benefits would be cut for workers who
chose to shift part of their payroll taxes to individual accounts but not
for those who refused the option. Governor Bush's campaign literature did not say how much of the payroll tax workers would be
allowed to shift, but he mentioned shifts of 2 to 5 percentage points.
Most discussion assumed a shift of 2 percentage points of the payroll
tax. Bush's literature also rejected using general revenues to bolster the
Social Security trust fund but left open whether general revenues
would be deposited in individual accounts.

Benefit Adequacy and Equity. The Bush principles would increase
the projected long-term deficit in the Social Security system by reducing payroll tax revenues. Exactly how much depends on how many
workers elect to divert part of their payroll taxes to individual
accounts. If one assumes that all workers elect the option, shifting 2
percentage points of the payroll tax starting in 2002 would increase the
projected long-term deficit (based on the actuary's 2000 projections)
from 1.89 percent of payroll to 3.8 percent of payroll. Because the
proposal protects benefits for the disabled and survivors and for current retirees and those near retirement, benefits accounting for about
two-fifths of the long-run cost of Social Security would be off-limits for
benefit cuts. That means that all of the reductions in benefits necessary
to lower costs by 3.8 percent of payroll would target retirement benefits for younger workers. As the following calculation illustrates, this
requirement implies benefit cuts averaging 41 percent over seventy-five
years for those benefits that are not protected.

     If anything, this estimate is conservative since, contrary to the
Bush principles, it assumes that survivor benefits for younger workers would be reduced. If that were not the case, the cuts in retirement benefits would be larger than 41 percent because the benefits
available for reductions would be smaller than those assumed in this

	Percent of taxable payroll
Estimated seventy-five-year cost of all Social Security benefits	15.4
Less: Estimated seventy-five-year cost of benefits that will not be cut	6.2
Equals: Cost of benefits available for reductions	9.2
Deficit after diverting 2 percentage points of the payroll tax	3.8
Cuts in unprotected benefits necessary to restore long-term balance if all workers open individual accounts	= 3.8/9.2 = 41 percent[7]

calculation. If more than 2 percentage points of payroll tax were diverted, the implied cuts in Social Security benefits would be correspondingly larger.

Of course, the cuts in Social Security benefits would be offset, at least in part, by benefits financed by individual accounts. The size of the offset would depend on how much was deposited in the accounts, the rate of return received on those accounts, and the length of time funds were left in the accounts. Older workers would have less time for their accounts to build up than would younger workers. As a result, the reduction in total retirement income—reduced Social Security plus pensions financed by individual accounts—would be larger for older than for younger workers if Social Security benefits for all workers below some age threshold were cut by the same percentage.

There are two ways to avoid unequal cuts in overall benefits. First, the cuts in Social Security benefits could be phased in. Older workers would experience smaller, younger workers larger, Social Security benefit cuts, so that the percentage reductions in total benefits—from the trimmed Social Security benefit plus the pensions based on individual account accumulations—would be equal for future retirees. Under this approach, Social Security benefit cuts would range from 25 percent for 55-year-old workers (assuming the proposal does not apply to older workers) to 54 percent for workers aged 30 or younger at the time the plan is implemented and for future young labor force entrants. The Social Security cuts would be offset, in part, by the pensions derived from the individual accounts, which would be larger for younger than for older workers. The second way to avoid cuts would be to transfer general revenues to individual accounts, causing them to grow more rapidly, or to the Social Security trust fund, thereby obviating the need for such large cuts in Social Security benefits.

Assuming historical average rates of return, the combined benefit from Social Security and the individual accounts would be cut relative to current law by 20 percent for single workers with average earnings histories. Cuts would be larger for low earners and for married couples and would be smaller for high earners. Many would see such a distribution of benefit cuts as unfair. This unfairness could be ameliorated by changing the Social Security benefit formula or by using general revenues to supplement transfers into the individual accounts of low earners.

The rate of return different cohorts of workers enjoyed on their individual accounts would determine the size of the total benefit cut each experienced. For single average earners whose returns equaled those over the worst thirty-five-year period since the advent of Social Security, total benefits would be cut 38 percent. If returns were as good as in the best thirty-five-year period, total benefits on the average would not be cut at all. Of course, regardless of average rates of return, some individual workers would have better luck or skill than others in selecting investments; as a result, some would gain and some would lose if workers were given wide choice of investments.

Benefits could be cut less if payroll taxes were raised or if general revenues were transferred to the Social Security system. But the Bush campaign explicitly pledged not to raise payroll taxes and said that the Gore proposal, which is examined below, to transfer general revenues to Social Security, "concealed" the projected long-term deficit. Nevertheless, Bush suggested that the Social Security trust fund could borrow when its reserves were depleted. Such borrowing only defers benefit cuts unless some other way is found to raise returns on Social Security reserves or general revenues are transferred into the system. This approach assumes that the trust fund would have the means to repay the loan. Suggestions that repayments could be made from higher corporate tax receipts, along the lines proposed in the Gramm-Domenici plan, are, as we pointed out, unrealistic. Moreover, a policy of borrowing to pay Social Security benefits would reduce saving and could provide unwanted fiscal stimulus to the economy.

General revenues could be transferred to individual accounts instead of to the trust fund. Such transfers could be done in a way to equalize the cuts in total benefits across age cohorts and speed the accumulation of individual account balances.[8] Benefits based on these enlarged accounts could offset or even eliminate *expected* cuts in Social Security benefits. But the greater the reliance on individual accounts, the greater the market and inflation risks to which workers are exposed. Without general revenue transfers to private accounts, the Bush proposal gets a low grade for adequacy. With general revenue transfers, adequacy can be maintained *on the average*, but workers would face financial market risks on a larger part of their retirement portfolio.

Protection against Risk. The Bush proposal ranks quite low on grounds of risk, at least for future retirement benefits. If the guarantee of survivor and disability benefits and of retirement pensions for those who are currently retired or soon will retire could be sustained in practice, the proposal would rank high on protecting *those* groups from risk. Future retirees would receive far smaller retirement benefits in a form protected from financial market fluctuations and from inflation. Instead, they would be more dependent on income from sources subject to market risk.

Although current retirees, those soon to retire, the disabled, and survivors seem to face no risks because the Bush proposal promises to sustain their benefits, this promise would create a dilemma for Congress. Elected officials would be loath to reduce secure Social Security benefits by 50 percent or more for young workers but entirely spare older workers, current retirees, the disabled, and survivors from any benefit cuts whatsoever. One possibility would be that Congress would decide that, if benefits are to be cut at all, most Americans should share the consequences. Alternatively, Congress could guarantee young workers a rate of return on their individual accounts sufficient to preclude more than minor overall cuts. Such a guarantee would create a large potential liability that future Congresses would be obliged to honor. The Social Security actuaries would doubtless put a price on such a guarantee, which would simply transform the acknowledged deficit in Social Security into a contingent debt to individual account holders.

Even more important than the direct financial risks that the Bush proposal would create are the political risks that it would engender should a significant minority of workers choose not to move part of their payroll taxes to individual accounts. High earners have more to gain from individual accounts than do low earners. The Social Security benefit formula, which favors low earners, means that high earners would forgo less than do low earners by accepting the lower benefits that they would be awarded if they shifted part of their payroll taxes to individual accounts. In addition, high earners typically invest in higher-yielding assets than do low earners. For these reasons, high earners are more likely than low earners to decide to shift payroll taxes to individual accounts.

But a disproportionate shift of payroll taxes by high earners would weaken Social Security's finances and necessitate additional benefit cuts or tax increases for those who remain under the system. The result could easily be the gradual erosion of Social Security. It is, perhaps, for this reason that Governor Bush acknowledged that his proposals were only the first step toward "a completely different world."[9]

Administrative Efficiency. The Bush proposal says nothing explicit about administrative arrangements, other than that participation in the diversion of payroll taxes to individual accounts would be voluntary. But the voluntary character of the plan raises serious administrative concerns. Would workers be able to decide year by year whether to divert payroll taxes to their individual accounts, or would they have to make a onetime election? Would they be able to choose among many, or just a few, investment accounts? Could they shift among investment accounts, and if so, how often? Would workers have to begin withdrawals at a particular age, or could they leave funds on deposit as long as they wish? What would happen to personal accounts at divorce? Governor Bush stated that individuals would be able to transfer unused portions of their individual accounts to heirs at death. This provision implied that annuitization would not be mandatory. If so, what would be done to prevent adverse selection from raising annuity prices for those who wished the protection of payments guaranteed to last until they died? Would the government provide indexed annuities if private markets did not?

Without answers to these and other questions, it is impossible to know how much the Bush proposal would increase administrative costs, how the plan would work, and even whether it would be administrable. If workers were required to make a onetime election to participate in the individual account plan, were permitted to choose among only a limited number of investment plans offering index funds, and were allowed to shift money among funds infrequently, administrative costs might be held to 30 to 40 basis points. The more choice workers are given regarding whether or not to contribute to individual accounts, what assets to invest in, and how frequently to reallocate their investments, the more costly administration would be. Under some variants, annual administrative costs could easily exceed 1 percent of funds on deposit, enough to consume 20 percent or more of potential accumulations over the full life of a pension plan.

National Saving. The basic principles of the Bush reform proposal imply that it would have no *direct* and immediate effect, positive or negative, on national saving. Transferring revenues from a government trust fund to an individual account simply relabels an asset. If benefits are cut to restore the balance between reduced payroll taxes and Social Security benefits—in the hope that benefits based on individual accounts will replace them—then saving would increase. Furthermore, if individual account balances earn higher returns than do Social Security reserves, and if individual account holders do not offset accumulating balances by reducing saving in other forms, the Bush proposal could boost saving in the long term.

Transferring general revenues to individual accounts also would raise saving, provided that the alternative to the transfer is government spending (which boosts collective consumption) or tax reductions (which largely go to private consumption). However, if the transfer is financed by public borrowing—that is, by increased government deficits or reduced surpluses—then it would not raise national saving. Each dollar added to private accounts would be offset by an additional dollar of government borrowing. Because Governor Bush called for tax cuts that would seriously deplete projected non–Social Security budget surpluses, any transfer of general revenues to individual accounts would have to be financed either by government borrowing or by spending reductions that he did not discuss during the campaign. For this reason, the Bush proposal is not likely to raise national saving. (See Table 7–5, page 152.)

THE GORE PROPOSALS

During his presidential campaign Vice President Gore embraced three modifications in Social Security. First, he proposed to transfer general revenues to the Social Security trust funds, starting in the year 2011, in amounts sufficient to reduce but not eliminate the projected long-term deficit. The transfers would be set to equal the drop in Treasury interest payments attributable to the reduction in publicly held debt made possible because of Social Security's cash flow

TABLE 7–5
REPORT CARD FOR THE
GEORGE W. BUSH SOCIAL SECURITY PRINCIPLES

CRITERIA	GRADE	
	Without general revenue transfers to individual accounts	With general revenue transfers to individual accounts
Adequacy, equity, and a fair return	D	A to C
Protection against risk	F	D
Administrative efficiency	B to F	B to F
Increased national saving	C–	C–
Overall grade	C– to D–	C+ to D+

surpluses between 2001 and 2015. These transfers would start at $122 billion in 2011 and rise to $257 billion in 2016 and later years.[10] They would reduce the projected long-term deficit from 1.89 percent of payroll to 0.86 percent of payroll, or 54 percent, according to Social Security actuaries.[11]

The Gore proposal also included two benefit liberalizations that would increase the projected long-term deficit. He recommended that benefits to surviving spouses be increased to 75 percent of the couple's combined benefit. But unlike our recommendation for increasing benefits for surviving spouses, which was described in Chapter 6, Gore did not recommend any reduction in the spouse's benefit itself. He also proposed to give earnings credits for up to five years to parents who remain at home with small children. The credits would be set at half of average covered earnings per worker, approximately $16,500 in 2001.

Outside of the framework of Social Security, Gore proposed a "Retirement Savings Plus" program. Under this initiative, low-, moderate-, and middle-income individuals who contribute $500 a year ($1,000 for couples) to qualified retirement savings accounts would receive matching payments from the federal government. The payments would take the form of tax credits, which could be deposited directly in the accounts. A credit of $3 would be given for each dollar saved by couples with incomes of $30,000 or less; $1 of credit would be provided for each dollar saved by couples with incomes of $30,000 to $60,000; and $1 of credit would be provided for each $3 saved by couples with incomes of $60,000 to $100,000. Income thresholds for single persons would be half those applicable to couples. After funds had been on deposit for five years, they would be available not only for retirement pensions but also to pay for college tuition, purchase of a first home, or defray large medical expenses.

Benefit Adequacy and Equity. Gore promised in general terms to sustain the current system. He also proposed two modest benefit increases and encouraged additional saving through individual accounts. As far as the proposal goes, it ranks high on benefit adequacy and equity. By promising to maintain the current benefit formula, which favors low earners, and to tilt tax credits in favor of households with modest incomes, the proposal ranks high on equity as well. Even if benefit cuts were used to complete the plan, it would rate high marks for guaranteeing a basic income to workers with modest earnings. But the proposal is incomplete because it does not explain how the projected long-term deficit would be closed.

Protection against Risk. By retaining the defined benefit structure of Social Security, the Gore proposal earns high marks for its commitment to protect workers from market risk. The separate Retirement Savings Plus accounts would be fully exposed to financial market risks. But all voluntary saving is risky. These accounts would be an additional layer atop a core defined-benefit system that assured benefits approximately equal to those promised under current law. In that the Gore plan does not provide a blueprint for ensuring the long-run solvency of Social Security, future retirees and taxpayers face some uncertainty and the risk that they may be adversely affected in unanticipated ways by whatever further reforms are enacted.

Administrative Efficiency. The Gore proposal would not require any changes in the low-cost administration of Social Security. The Retirement Savings Plus accounts would be costly to administer, however. The tax credit mechanism could work in either of two ways. Workers could designate on their tax forms whether they had contributed to qualified savings accounts and name the recipient institution so that the Treasury could deposit the requisite credit. Or financial institutions could report yearly to the Treasury contributions made by account holders, and the Treasury could send the appropriate-sized credit after checking the individual's income using tax records. Under either approach, the paperwork burden would be significant, auditing would be both important and difficult, and the hurdles to participation facing those not required to file an income tax return would be high. This part of the Gore proposal would be very cumbersome to administer, and so it gets a low grade in this area.

National Saving. The Gore proposal would tend to boost national saving. Like Governor Bush and most members of Congress, Gore promises not to use Social Security surpluses to finance tax cuts or non-Social Security spending increases. The general revenue transfers to Social Security, like the proposed transfers of general revenues in other plans, would boost national saving if the alternative to the transfers was tax cuts or spending increases but not if the alternative was maintenance of federal budget surpluses. Retirement Savings Plus accounts would add to national saving to the extent that deposits in such accounts represented new private saving and the tax credits substituted for tax cuts or spending increases. Much of the private saving probably would be new, because the credits would encourage saving by individuals and couples who currently save little or nothing.

In the end, however, the grade on the Gore proposals must be an incomplete, as the plan does not meet the standard of restoring long-term financial balance. It is worth noting, however, that if the Retirement Saving Plus accounts prove to be wildly popular, the retirement assets available to many of those who had low and moderate incomes during their working years could rise significantly. This could reduce political opposition to modest Social Security benefits cuts when the system faced insolvency in the last half of the twenty-first century. Under such circumstances, those who did not avail themselves of the opportunity to have their savings subsidized by tax credits could end up with inadequate incomes in retirement. (See Table 7–6.)

TABLE 7–6
REPORT CARD FOR THE
AL GORE SOCIAL SECURITY PROPOSALS

CRITERIA	GRADE (SOCIAL SECURITY/ SOCIAL SECURITY AND SAVINGS PLUS)
Adequacy, equity, and a fair return	Incomplete (A–/A–)
Protection against risk	Incomplete (B+)
Administrative efficiency	A/D
Increased national saving	A/A
Overall grade	Incomplete

SOCIAL SECURITY MODERNIZATION PLAN

The plan we described in Chapter 6 relies exclusively on defined-benefit retirement pensions. The distinctive characteristic of this plan is that it closes the projected long-term deficit equally through benefit reductions and increased revenues. Moreover, the plan goes beyond fiscal balance to achieve a modest surplus in projected long-term finances. It would build a large trust fund that would persist indefinitely, generating interest income to supplement unchanged payroll tax rates. It envisages the creation of a new, private Fiduciary Corporation (FC), an institution that could manage investment not only of the part of Social Security reserves held in private securities but also of the federal government's positive balances that will begin to grow once the debt held by the public has been repaid, assuming the budget remains in surplus. The operations of the Social Security system would be removed from the budget presentations of the executive and legislative branches. The FC would be charged with achieving, over the course of several decades, reserve balances equal to the "open-group" liability of the Social Security system—that is, balances equal to the present value of the difference between revenues (from payroll taxes, other earmarked taxes, and general revenue transfers) and expenditures. The trust funds' investments would be diversified among government bonds and private stocks and bonds.

In addition, we propose that benefits increase at a slower rate than is called for under the current benefit formula. Under current law, initial benefits rise with average wages and, once computed, they are adjusted yearly for inflation. Our proposed "cuts" would still permit new benefits to rise but more slowly than average wages. The benefit cuts would be designed to reflect the changes that have occurred in the labor force and in life expectancy since the program was enacted.

Benefit Adequacy and Equity. This plan reduces benefits somewhat, but it does not cut pensions significantly below those promised in current law for such vulnerable groups as the disabled. Most surviving spouses would experience a small increase in benefits relative to current law. Benefits for retired couples in which one spouse had little or no earnings history, on the other hand, would decline modestly relative to current law. By investing some of the trust funds' reserves in a diversified portfolio, the plan would bring to people dependent on public pensions the higher yields that a broad portfolio of public and private bonds and stocks makes possible.

Protection against Risk. The Social Security Modernization Plan preserves the key advantage of defined-benefit pension plans by spreading risks broadly among the general population. Benefits would remain fully protected from inflation. Because the plan more than closes the currently projected deficit, system adjustments would not be necessary even if the economy grew less rapidly than assumed. Furthermore, the plan incorporates a mechanism that would help to ensure that if the reformed program were to fall out of long-run actuarial balance in the future, policymakers would enact corrective measures.

Administrative Efficiency. This plan maintains all the administrative efficiencies of the current system.

National Saving. This plan would add to national saving. It would somewhat slow the rate of growth of benefit outlays. The general revenue transfers would forestall use of emerging budget surpluses for current consumption, private or public, through tax cuts or increased government spending. The plan would further isolate Social Security surpluses from the general budget process thereby enhancing the likelihood that they would add to national saving.

Nobody will be surprised if we award the plan we sketched out in Chapter 6 the top overall grade, an A–. That plan best meets the criteria we set forth earlier in this chapter. (See Table 7–7.)

TABLE 7–7
REPORT CARD FOR THE
SOCIAL SECURITY MODERNIZATION PLAN

CRITERIA	GRADE
Adequacy, equity, and a fair return	B+
Protection against risk	A
Administrative efficiency	A
Increased national saving	A–
Overall grade	A–

CONCLUSION

No perfect way exists to reform the nation's mandatory retirement program; all plans involve tradeoffs among desirable objectives. Table 7–8 (page 158) is our "grade sheet" for the six plans. We did not give our plan a straight A because we think no plan that cuts benefits or raises taxes merits that grade. Furthermore, our plan— like all others—contains politically unpopular provisions that elected officials will find hard to endorse.

While we have argued that a strong case exists for general revenue transfers to close the entire projected long-term deficit, we believe that such a policy would be unwise. So large a commitment of future federal revenues would represent a heavy charge against the budget and could unduly restrict the capacity of future lawmakers to respond to new social and economic challenges. But shifting some of the burden of the unfunded liability from future workers and beneficiaries to the general taxpayer is fair. The nation as a whole created those liabilities through explicit decisions to pay the early generations of Social Security participants benefits that far exceeded

TABLE 7–8
SUMMARY REPORT CARD

PLAN	GRADE
Archer-Shaw Plan	B
Gramm-Domenici Plan	C–
Breaux-Gregg Plan	C+
Bush Principles	C–/D
Gore Proposal	Incomplete
Social Security Modernization Plan	A–

those justified by their modest payroll tax contributions. The nation as a whole also benefited from these decisions; millions of parents, grandparents, and great-grandparents of today's workers were able to lead dignified, independent lives as a consequence of their adequate Social Security pensions. We think, therefore, that the nation as a whole should pay for at least some of those liabilities in the same way it pays other general obligations—through general revenues.

Investing Social Security's growing reserves, collectively or through individual accounts, in assets that have higher yields than government bonds can help close the projected long-term deficit. But that policy change alone will not be enough. To finish the job, future retirees will have to accept smaller benefits than those promised under current law or future workers will have to pay higher taxes. The weight lifter's maxim, "no pain, no gain," applies also to pension policy. The question is: Whose gain and whose pain?

APPENDIX TO CHAPTER 7

FEATURES OF THE ARCHER-SHAW
SOCIAL SECURITY GUARANTEE PLAN

GENERAL CHANGES

◆ Supplements revenue inflow with a payment of 2 percent of taxable earnings into Social Security Guarantee Account from the general budget surplus.

BENEFIT CHANGES

◆ Full benefits, including COLAs, remain guaranteed.

◆ Benefits increase to those whose SSGA accumulation is sufficient to provide an annuity larger than their current calculated Social Security benefit (estimated to be about 5 percent of individual account accumulations.

REVENUE CHANGES

◆ Tax credits into SSGAs financed by transfers from the general budget.

◆ Payroll tax will be phased down from 12.4 percent to 9.9 percent in 2050, and again to 8.9 percent in 2060.

PERSONAL ACCOUNTS

◆ Establishes individual Social Security Guarantee Accounts through an annual refundable income tax credit equal to 2 percent of a worker's wages subject to payroll tax, financed by funds from the general budget surplus.

◆ Once workers reach retirement or become disabled, the amount in their SSGA is transferred to the Social Security trust fund. An annuity is calculated based on the accrued assets in their individual SSGA. If the annuity is larger than the Social Security benefit, they receive that amount. If it is smaller than the Social Security benefit, they receive the Social Security benefit.

◆ Balances of workers who die prior to retirement can be passed tax-free to heirs, provided that no potential dependent or survivor beneficiaries exist. In all other cases, balances flow entirely to the Social Security trust fund.

FEATURES OF THE GRAMM-DOMENICI
SOCIAL SECURITY PRESERVATION PLAN

GENERAL CHANGES

- Redirects 3 percentage points of the current 12.4 percent payroll tax into individual accounts, which are invested in private funds.

BENEFIT CHANGES

- During the transition phase, benefits are guaranteed to equal Social Security benefits, plus 20 percent of the annuity computed based on the amount accumulated in worker's private account.
- Once the transition has been completed (2045), benefits will be guaranteed to be 120 percent of current Social Security benefit.
- According to projections, once the program has been fully implemented, the investments will yield benefits two and one-half times larger than those of the current system.

REVENUE CHANGES

- Program will be financed by:
- Transfers from the general budget surplus
- Redeeming 72 percent of the current Social Security trust fund
- Projected corporate tax revenues resulting from increased private investment
- Payroll tax will gradually be phased down from 12.4 percent to 10 percent (8.5 percent Social Security, 1.5 percent Disability Insurance).

PERSONAL ACCOUNTS

- Current workers are given the option to create a Social Security Individual Investment Account (SI Account).
- New workers are automatically entered into the new system.
- In the new system, 3 percentage points of the current payroll tax are invested in a worker's private SI Account. The remaining 9.4 percent of the current payroll tax continues to be fed into the existing Social Security system.
- At retirement, an annuity is calculated based on the amount accrued in the account.
- Balances of workers who die prior to retirement can be passed tax-free to heirs, with the present value of all dependent and survivor benefits deducted.

FEATURES OF THE BREAUX-GREGG TWENTY-FIRST CENTURY RETIREMENT PLAN

GENERAL CHANGES

+ All newly hired state and local workers would be covered.
+ The early retirement penalty and the delayed retirement credit would be increased to make them more accurate.

BENEFIT CHANGES

+ A minimum benefit would be established equal to 60 percent of the poverty threshold for those with twenty years of covered earnings and rising by 2 percentage points per additional year to 100 percent of the poverty threshold for those with forty or more years of covered earnings.
+ The age at which unreduced benefits are paid would be increased two months a year, reaching age 70 in 2029, and by one month every year and a half thereafter, reaching 72 in 2065.
+ The spouse's benefit would be gradually reduced from one-half to one-third of the primary worker's benefit.
+ Benefits would be computed by summing all of a worker's adjusted earnings and dividing by forty.
+ Benefits would be reduced gradually for all newly retired workers with average adjusted lifetime earnings above about $6,372 (in 2000 and adjusted upward by the growth in average wages).
+ The annual cost-of-living adjustment would be reduced to account for a portion of the bias remaining in the measured CPI.

REVENUE CHANGES

+ Two percentage points of the current 12.4 percent payroll tax would be diverted to individual accounts.

PERSONAL ACCOUNTS

+ Personal accounts similar in investment options and management to accounts held in the federal employees' Thrift Savings Plan (see Box 6–5) would be established using 2 percentage points of the existing payroll tax. Supplemental voluntary contributions of up to $2,000 per year would be permitted.
+ Upon retirement, a portion of the accounts' balances would have to be used to purchase an inflation-protected annuity that, when added to the scaled back Social Security benefit, met a minimum threshold for retirement income adequacy. Excess balances could be withdrawn according to the retiree's needs.

FEATURES OF THE BUSH SOCIAL SECURITY PRINCIPLES

BENEFIT CHANGES

- Benefits for the disabled and survivors, as well as for current retirees and those near retirement, will not change.
- Benefits for younger workers would be reduced, as would be benefits for those who choose to shift part of their payroll taxes to individual accounts.

REVENUE CHANGES

- Some of the current 12.4 percent payroll tax shifted to individual accounts at worker's option.

PERSONAL ACCOUNTS

- Workers permitted but not required to shift a portion of their payroll taxes from the Social Security trust funds into individual accounts.
- Workers may transfer individual account accumulations to heirs at death.

FEATURES OF THE GORE SOCIAL SECURITY PROPOSALS

GENERAL CHANGES

* Maintains the current system, supplementing revenue with transfers from the general budget surplus.

BENEFIT CHANGES

* Increases benefits to surviving spouses (to 75 percent of the couple's combined benefit).
* Establishes earnings credit (set at half of average covered earnings per worker) for up to five years for parents who remain at home with small children.

REVENUE CHANGES

* Transfers general revenues to the Social Security trust funds.

PERSONAL ACCOUNTS

* Establishes a Retirement Savings Plus program (entirely separate from the Social Security program).
  - The government matches individual deposits into these accounts at different rates based on income level. The proposed matching rates are $3 of credit for $1 saved by a couple earning $30,000 or less; $1 of credit for $1 saved by couples with incomes of $30,000 to $60,000; and $1 of credit for $3 saved by couples earning $60,000 to $100,000.
  - Once funds have been on deposit for five years, they can be withdrawn not only for retirement but also for college tuition, a first home, or large medical expenses.

8

THE POLITICS OF REFORM

If references to Social Security as the third rail of American politics were once valid, someone has turned off the electricity. Proposals to replace Social Security, in part or in whole, with individually owned private accounts or to deposit general revenues in the Social Security trust funds, once regarded as beyond the political pale, became centerpieces in the campaigns of the two major candidates for president in 2000.

But in truth, Social Security was never untouchable. Congress significantly curtailed Social Security benefits twice over the past quarter of a century—in 1977 and 1983. None of the elected officials who supported these cuts suffered political electrocution. Most people back then accepted benefit cuts and tax increases because they were seen as necessary to restore the program's financial integrity. There is no reason to believe that the public will respond differently now to sacrifice if people are convinced that belt-tightening is needed to ensure that future Social Security pensions for the elderly and disabled are secure and adequate.

The one occasion when elected officials did receive a high-voltage jolt was in 1982. In that year, President Reagan proposed large cuts in retirement, survivor's, and disability benefits that would have taken effect just a few months after enactment. No member of the Senate could be found to sponsor the president's plan. This experience, flowing from an ill-considered proposal, gave rise to the vivid but inaccurate "third-rail" metaphor. The vital political lesson suggested by the complete record, however, is that Congresses and presidents can address the program's problems without fear of political retribution if the public understands that action is necessary to maintain a stable, fair, and adequate retirement system. Even then, it helps if a sizable contingent from both political parties engages in the effort so that neither party later can waylay the other for "betraying the elderly."

Whether conditions are now ripe for action is unclear. Social Security is far from collapse. The program's receipts now exceed expenditures by more than $150 billion a year. Surpluses will persist for at least two decades. And Social Security's financial prospects have been improving since 1997. But the public increasingly has become aware that, if current projections are not far off the mark, the retirement of the baby boomers will raise costs and eventually push the program into deficit, that the program's projected long-term deficit must eventually be closed, and that prompt action can forestall a later crisis. President Clinton's call during the 1998 State of the Union address for a national discussion on how best to strengthen the program for the long run received bipartisan commendation. Furthermore, most senators and representatives have discussed Social Security's long-run problems in a forthright manner. Many have introduced or cosponsored bills that address Social Security's fiscal imbalance—through substantial benefit reductions, tax increases, and radical structural reforms. No one has been punished at the voting booth. The 2000 campaign for the presidency has further advanced the debate and enhanced public understanding of the long-run problem and the alternative solutions. As yet, however, appreciation of the difficult trade-offs that will have to be made is not widespread.

The emergence of favorable economic conditions—budget surpluses, low unemployment, and low inflation—also has improved the environment for reform. When the budget was in deficit, those pushing for benefit cuts or payroll tax increases to strengthen Social Security were vulnerable to the charge that they were trying to balance the overall budget, pay for income tax cuts, or finance a favorite expenditure program by restraining Social Security. Now that the non-Social Security budget, as well as Social Security, are in surplus, the tables have turned. Most recent reform proposals call for transferring a portion of the non-Social Security budget surplus to the trust funds or for using it to fund individual accounts.

The 2000 elections ended six years of divided government. But the passage of significant Social Security reforms will require substantial bipartisan support. For starters, any forty senators can filibuster a plan with which they strongly disagree. With the Senate equally divided, each party would have to secure at least ten members of the opposition to cut off debate. More importantly, both parties realize that far-reaching modifications of a program, such as Social Security, that deeply affect virtually every American family would be too dangerous to undertake without bipartisan support.

Republicans and Democrats will find it hard to agree whether to modify the structure of Social Security and how to close the projected long-run deficit. A major obstacle will be the steadily improving financial condition of Social Security. In 1997, the program's actuary projected that the trust funds would be exhausted in 2029. By 2000, the exhaustion date had moved out to 2037, and the size of the projected long-term deficit had fallen from 2.23 percent of payroll to 1.89 percent.

Faced with a problem whose severity seems to be shrinking, many elected officials will argue that "watchful waiting" is the prudent response, that hasty action is unnecessary, and that more study and analysis is desirable. Others will point out that the same strong economy that has reduced the projected long-term deficit has generated an unexpected and probably short-lived opportunity in the form of large non-Social Security budget surpluses. These surpluses, they argue, could be used to restore balance in the current system or to fund new individual accounts without resorting to significant payroll tax increases or benefit reductions.

A larger hurdle to seizing this unique opportunity is the philosophical chasm that separates those who want to retain the current defined-benefit system and those who want to replace it in whole or in part with a system of individually managed private accounts. These differences are exacerbated by a failure of many participants in the debate to understand fully the technical issues of pension design. In addition, crass considerations of political advantage will have to be overcome.

As Americans weigh the merits of alternative reforms, they should not lose sight of two political questions about every plan:

+ Can it be enacted now?

+ Can it be sustained?

POLITICAL SUPPORT FOR ENACTMENT

However high a plan may rank on our criteria for reform, it is no more than an intellectual toy if it cannot generate the political support needed to pass Congress and secure the president's signature well before the retirement of the baby boomers is in full swing. In particular, a politically viable plan requires at least grudging acceptance from most of the parties that have an important stake in Social Security reform, including:

+ workers, whose interests will vary depending on age, earnings, family circumstances, and whether they participate in a private pension plan;

+ unions;

+ employers, whose views may depend on the size, wage level, and stability of their workforce; whether they offer a pension plan, and, if they do, the extent to which that plan is integrated with Social Security; and the degree to which their payroll and benefit systems are automated;

+ governors, congressional representatives, state legislators, and civil servants from states that have elected to remain outside the Social Security system;

+ the retired and organizations that represent them; and

+ a wide range of business and civic groups concerned about the nation's mandatory retirement system.

None of these groups has an absolute veto, but loud, vigorous opposition from any will cause some members of Congress to oppose a particular proposal and make other members cautious about endorsing major changes in Social Security. To weld a majority coalition for reform will require the president to participate actively in the debate and strike deals in order to bring along reluctant members of Congress.

MEASURES TO CLOSE DEFICITS ARE NEVER POPULAR

The effort to close the overall federal deficit that occupied Congress and successive presidents from 1983 until 1999 made it clear that raising taxes or cutting spending is never easy and rarely popular. There is nothing like good luck, in the form of unexpectedly robust economic growth, larger than anticipated tax collections, and the sudden collapse of the nation's primary military adversary to make the job easier. But what would "good luck" mean in the context of Social Security reform? Could it spare politicians the difficult decisions?

COULD THE PROJECTIONS BE WRONG?

The projections of the Social Security actuaries are regularly attacked as overly pessimistic by advocates of the status quo and as overly optimistic by advocates of radical change. Both are probably right in detail but wrong in their overall evaluations. The projections are based on a number of assumptions regarding variables that are notoriously difficult to forecast. Current assumptions all fall within the range of views held by responsible private experts who make their livelihoods forecasting long-run demographic, labor market, and economic conditions. The political debate should accept these projections as reasonable and the best available indications of the future.

But, as the Congressional Budget Office's ten-year estimates of balance in the unified federal budget have shown, even methodologically sophisticated, nonpartisan projections can be quite unreliable. For example, in 1995, CBO projected that the unified budget would be in deficit by roughly $420 billion in 2005 if policy remained unchanged. Five years later, in 2000, CBO estimated that a surplus of approximately $520 billion would occur in 2005 if the policies of

2000 were still in place in that year. This huge difference in estimated budget balance—nearly $1 trillion for the single year 2005—reflects the effects of unanticipated changes in the strength of the economy and, to a lesser extent, technical factors and revised expectations about the economy's future performance. Over longer periods of time, small changes in assumptions about the economy or other issues, such as the underlying growth rate of medical costs, can have huge impacts. For example, CBO's long-run projections of spending in 2040 on items other than Social Security and interest vary by more than 10 percent of GDP depending on whether optimistic or pessimistic assumptions are used for the growth of productivity, population, and health costs.[1]

The projected long-term Social Security balance is nowhere near as volatile as that of the unified budget. Nevertheless, the actuary's projections are far from certain. Without any significant changes to policy, the projected long-term deficit in Social Security grew gradually from a *de minimis* level in 1983 until 1997 and then shrank somewhat through the year 2000.

Uncertain though projections may be, lawmakers should not procrastinate, hoping that they will be spared the unpleasant task of cutting benefits or raising taxes—it is highly unlikely that good luck will serve up a political free lunch.

TAX INCREASES

U.S. taxes are low by international standards. Nonetheless, neither party has shown any interest in using payroll tax increases to close the projected long-term Social Security deficit. In fact, both candidates in the 2000 presidential campaign pledged not to raise payroll tax rates. Elected officials and the general public have displayed some interest in increasing the proportion of earnings subject to the payroll tax. A modest increase in the earnings base, so that the tax covers 90 percent of earnings, would reduce the projected long-term deficit by about 25 percent. Such an increase would reduce the need to rely on benefit cuts or general revenue transfers to reform Social Security, as would a small increase in payroll tax rates. Some plans try to overcome opposition to higher taxes by earmarking the added revenues for personal accounts and by exempting employers from the new tax.

COST-OF-LIVING ADJUSTMENTS

Proposals to reduce annual cost-of-living adjustments will—and we think should—provoke powerful opposition. For many years, the consumer price index (CPI) overstated inflation. The Bureau of Labor Statistics has implemented some corrections that have greatly reduced this bias. A few additional changes might be made; such changes tend to be difficult to implement, however, and we have not included any possible savings from them in our estimates. The CPI should be made as accurate as possible, but we see no justification for failing to compensate pensioners fully for inflation. Moreover, spokespersons for the elderly and disabled will protest loudly that denial of full inflation adjustments cumulates over time, creating real hardship, and they are right. Thus, we believe that the full cost-of-living adjustment should be retained.

If full cost-of-living adjustments are denied to Social Security beneficiaries, it would be hard politically to sustain other cost-of-living adjustments, including those in the tax code and in other popular programs that are adjusted annually by the CPI such as those for veterans, retired civil servants, and recipients of student loans. In the tax code, annual inflation adjustments increase personal exemptions, the standard deduction, and the amount of income subject to the various tax rates. This connection between cost-of-living adjustments in Social Security and similar adjustments in other programs makes any denial of full adjustment unlikely.

HOW MANY VOTES DO THEY HAVE?

Joseph Stalin cynically derided the importance of the papacy during World War II by asking, "How many divisions does the Pope have?" A contemporary cynic might ask us and other policy analysts how many votes we have for the various analytically sound, but politically unappealing, reforms that we recommend. However strong the case may be for extending Social Security to all new state and local workers, for taxing Social Security benefits like private pensions, and for increasing the age at which unreduced benefits are paid, opinion polls reveal very little support for these policies. Extending coverage would provide state and local employees with better disability, survivor's, and spouse's benefits, as well as improved pension protection against inflation. But many representatives from currently uncovered states—which happen to include such political heavyweights as California, Texas, Massachusetts, and Ohio—will oppose extending coverage. They understand that the average earnings of their state's employees exceed average Social Security earnings. By maintaining separate retirement systems, these states can avoid some of the costs of the assistance Social Security provides to low earners. They also can avoid responsibility for paying part of the unfunded liability that all covered workers sooner or later will be required to shoulder. Affected jurisdictions will argue that integrating their pension plans for new hires with Social Security is an impossibly complex task. The fact that the federal government brought all its new employees into Social Security starting in 1984 indicates that this argument is substantively weak but may not impair its political potency.

Extending to Social Security benefits the same personal income tax rules that apply to other contributory pensions makes sense. Once again, however, the opposition to such a tax change is strong—among middle- and upper-middle-income retirees, because they would have to pay higher taxes, and among those who oppose tax increases in any shape or form. High-income retirees have little at stake, because legislation enacted in 1983 and 1993 already subjects their benefits to tax. Personal exemptions and the standard deduction would continue to shield benefits of low-income retirees from tax. Middle- and upper-middle-income beneficiaries, however, would face higher taxes. Retirees who count on this tax-favored income are not likely to be mollified because most of the benefits they receive represent returns far in excess of the payroll taxes they paid as individuals and because such returns are routinely taxed when they come through contributory private pensions.

Finally, some benefit cuts will be needed to avoid significant payroll tax increases, unless lawmakers are willing to close most of the projected long-term deficit though large general revenue infusions and investment of reserves in higher-yielding assets. Polls indicate that the public thinks current benefits are, if anything, too low and does not want to see them cut. Elected officials read polls—and their mail. No matter what form a benefit cut takes, it runs afoul of the political Hippocratic oath—"at least do no *visible* harm"—and supporting votes will be hard to come by.

A KEY PRINCIPLE—MAKE HASTE SLOWLY

These and other potential flashpoints of opposition may be defused by lengthy phase-in periods. President Reagan ran into a firestorm in 1982 when he proposed benefit cuts that would have taken effect only a few months after enactment. Yet Congress subsequently found far larger changes acceptable, in part because they were phased in gradually. Specifically, Congress in 1983 cut benefits relative to prior law roughly 13 percent by raising the age at which unreduced benefits are paid from 65 to 67. At the same time, it deferred the first changes until the year 2000 and then spread them over the next twenty-two years. Similarly, while OASDI payroll tax rates have been raised from 9.2 to 12.4 percent of covered earnings since 1971, and additional increases have been made in the portion of earnings subject to tax, the increases came in nine small hikes, none larger than 0.72 percentage points and four of them 0.2 percentage points or less.

SUSTAINING POLITICAL SUPPORT

Social Security is too large and important to the economy and too central to the lives of millions of individuals to undergo frequent change. If participants are to make rational lifetime personal saving plans, they need to know that the core structure of the nation's basic retirement program will remain stable. Employers whose private pension plans supplement the mandatory public system want a public pension system that is not in constant flux. Political sustainability is a vital attribute of any reform plan. A plan that contains the political seeds of its own demise or encourages continued transformation is therefore a bad plan.

The current system has passed the test of political sustainability summa cum laude. It has generated powerful—some would say, excessive—support for its preservation. Workers who have paid taxes for years come to feel that they have an earned right to receive pensions in the promised amounts when they become old or disabled. While advocates of change may wish the current system elicited a bit less support, no program that fails to develop and maintain loyal political allegiance can long survive in a democracy.

Proposals to base a retirement pension system on private accounts are likely to fail the durability test for several reasons. First, keeping funds locked up until workers retire will be hard. The history of Individual Retirement Accounts (IRAs) is illustrative. Over time, pressures have mounted to permit individuals to gain access to IRA balances before retirement. Congress has succumbed to those pressures, giving individuals access to these accounts under a lengthening list of conditions. Similar pressures are certain to arise with respect to any individual accounts. Workers could increasingly come to view these accounts as similar to other private saving vehicles. The first step would be permission to use the accounts to pay for major medical expenses, then to pay for first-time home purchases, education, or living expenses during extended unemployment. Each new and worthy use would further undermine the primary goal of ensuring adequate retirement income. Vice President Gore implicitly recognized these pressures by building withdrawal options into his Retirement Savings Plus proposal, a program that he did not integrate with Social Security.

The inevitable ups and downs of financial markets also are likely to jeopardize the stability of a system based on personal accounts. Figure 3-1 showed that the value of pensions that individual accounts could support would have fallen more than 60 percent between 1969 and 1976 if reserves were invested in common stocks. Similar, if somewhat smaller, risks threaten funds invested in long-term bonds. Congress would face overwhelming pressures to intervene to protect investments or to provide supplements for cohorts whose replacement rates were smaller than those of earlier cohorts. Such bailouts would transform individual accounts into something quite different from what current advocates are now proposing. Whether or not such hybrids would be desirable, the full ramifications of individual accounts should be considered before any action is taken to create them.

All plans that combine traditional Social Security with new private accounts contain an element of political risk. The personal accounts component of such hybrid systems would pay a return equal to the yield of whatever assets depositors chose for their portfolios. The traditional Social Security component would seem to provide workers with smaller benefits per dollar of payroll taxes than do personal accounts. The reason is that most payroll taxes paid to Social Security are used to support benefits for previous retirees. In addition, some of the taxes paid by high earners would go to support the social functions of Social Security—the extra benefits for low earners and families with children. None of the taxes deposited into personal accounts would be siphoned off for these purposes.

Because Social Security would continue to bear responsibility for supporting past retirees and providing social assistance, it would appear to generate lower returns, especially for middle and high earners, even if the trust funds earned returns as high as or higher than those of individual accounts. After comparing the returns on personal accounts with the apparent yield offered by Social Security, many workers would conclude that they could do better if they were permitted to shift payroll taxes from Social Security to their individual accounts. The conclusion would be false, as we showed in Chapter 5, because workers would have to keep supporting benefits for current retirees. But the threat to the viability of Social Security would be real. It is doubtful whether such a system would be politically sustainable.

Barring general revenue transfers, there is no way that Social Security can fulfill its social functions without depressing the rate of return high earners receive on their Social Security contributions. Partial privatization plans expose and underscore the unavoidable conflict of objectives and could, over time, threaten continued fulfillment of the program's social functions. After exercising their option to shift some of their payroll taxes into individual accounts, high earners would quickly realize that they could do even better if they were allowed to shift even more of their payroll taxes to their personal accounts. The political consensus on behalf of providing relatively large benefits to low and moderate earners would weaken, threatening the survival of those benefits over the long-term. A central question about partial privatization plans, therefore, is whether they would protect low earners *in practice* as well as they appear to do *on paper*. Those who support Social Security in part because it has created a stable and mutually supportive coalition on behalf of pensions for everyone and social assistance for low earners have reason to be concerned that various individual account proposals would put social assistance in jeopardy.

CONCLUSION

America has a rare opportunity to restore financial balance to the nation's mandatory retirement system and to modernize it for the twenty-first century. The economy is strong. Inflation is under control.

Non–Social Security budget surpluses can be used to shift some of the burden for paying down the unfunded liability with general revenues rather than with increased payroll taxes or reduced benefits. Demographic pressures are currently low; the proportion of the population that is age 62 or older will rise little between 2000 and 2008—from 14.9 percent to 15.6 percent.

These favorable circumstances will not last. The leading edge of the baby-boom generation will reach retirement age in 2008. In 2019, almost twice as many people will turn 62 as did in 1999. As the baby boomers retire, spending on Social Security, Medicare, Supplemental Security Income, and Medicaid will rise rapidly. Current projections indicate that today's budget surpluses may be replaced by growing deficits unless future obligations are curtailed or taxes are increased.

Both current and future conditions make prompt action to reform Social Security highly desirable. As more baby boomers retire, the politics of reform will become increasingly difficult and the options more circumscribed. But early action does not mean that speedy implementation is desirable. Social Security is running large cash flow surpluses and will continue to do so for many years. The economy is performing better than assumed in the long-term actuarial projections, raising the prospect that the long-run deficits projected in the actuary's reports will continue to shrink over the next few years. But recent good fortune could end. It is important now to legislate phased changes, scheduled to take effect in the future, which could be reversed if strong economic performance continues and increased if projected deficits increase. These changes should be sufficient to restore projected long-term financial balance—and even better, to produce projected surpluses. If nothing is done until exhaustion of the trust funds is imminent, payroll tax increases will become the only realistic option. Early action to close the projected long-term deficits of Social Security permits adoption of other changes that can be phased in gradually and reversed if they are not needed. Delay is politically tempting—why enact benefits or raise taxes when current revenues continue to exceed expenditures? But delay would be a mistake, narrowing options and making future actions more wrenching.

NOTES

1

1. These estimates assume that the earnings of the 30-year-old rise 3 percent more than inflation each year, the return on saving is 5 percent more than inflation, and the individual dies at age 85. For information on retirement saving and stated retirement intentions of various age groups, see Employee Benefit Research Institute, *The 2000 Retirement Confidence Survey and RCS Minority Survey*, Washington, D.C., 2000, http://www.ebri.org/rcs/2000/2000_results.htm.

2. Annamaria Lusardi, "Information, Expectations, and Saving for Retirement," in Henry J. Aaron, ed., *Behavioral Dimensions of Retirement Economics* (Washington, D.C.: Brookings Institution, 1999), pp. 81–115.

3. Employee Benefit Research Institute, *2000 Retirement Confidence Survey and RCS Minority Survey*.

4. Support for the indigent may also promote excessively risky investment behavior by those with modest assets. Suppose that accumulated saving will provide a retirement income slightly greater than public aid if invested in a responsible mix of assets. One may be tempted to make a chancy investment with a small prospect of a big return, safe in the knowledge that if it succeeds, one reaps the gain, but if it fails one loses little, as one can fall back on public aid.

5. The creation of private accounts does not necessarily increase saving. For example, private accounts could be "funded" if the government deposited bonds in those accounts, but this step would add nothing to

national saving. Similarly, shifting payroll taxes to private accounts would not increase national saving if the shift reduced surpluses that otherwise would have accrued to the Social Security trust funds.

6. Arthur B. Kennickell et al., "Recent Changes in U.S. Family Finances: Results from the 1998 Survey of Consumer Finances," *Federal Reserve Bulletin* 86, no. 1 (January 2000): 1–29; also http://www.federalreserve.gov/pubs/bulletin/2000/0100lead.pdf .

2

1. W. Andrew Achenbaum, *Social Security: Visions and Revisions* (New York: Cambridge University Press, 1986), p. 18; Edward O. Berkowitz, *America's Welfare State: From Roosevelt to Reagan* (Baltimore: Johns Hopkins University Press, 1991), p. 19.

2. By 1975, however, the law had been liberalized many times. Coverage was greatly extended in 1950. Disability benefits were added in 1956. Workers retiring in 1975 who had benefited from these and other liberalizations had not spent their full working lives paying taxes under the system from which they drew benefits. Accordingly, workers actually retiring in 1975 continued to receive benefits worth far more than the value of taxes they and their employers had paid.

3. Aid to Dependent Children (ADC) reimbursed states for a share of the costs they incurred providing welfare benefits to children living in fatherless families. It was renamed Aid to Families with Dependent Children (AFDC) in 1962 to reflect the fact that in 1950 the adult caregivers of these children became eligible for benefits. In 1996, the AFDC program was replaced with the Temporary Assistance to Needy Families (TANF) program.

4. Until the 1950s, reserves grew rapidly despite the policy change, because wages and employment grew rapidly during and after World War II and because benefits were not adjusted automatically for inflation. Starting in 1950, Congress periodically raised benefits by about the same amount that earnings increased, so that revenues, which were based on earnings, did not outpace benefits.

5. While the regular unemployment compensation program provides benefits for up to six months, Congress has often extended assistance for a year or more during periods of economic weakness.

6. Reduced Social Security benefits for those age 62 to 64 were made available to women in 1957 and men in 1962.

7. Frank Levy, *Dollars and Dreams: The Changing American Income Distribution* (New York: W.W. Norton & Co., 1988).

3

1. Whether workers' earnings grow steadily, rapidly at first and then slowly, or slowly at first and then rapidly will have a significant effect on the size of a defined-contribution pension relative to workers' final wages. Take, for example, three cases in which workers' earnings grew at an average rate of 5 percent over their forty-year careers. If earnings grew at 8.1 percent during the first twenty years and 2 percent during the second twenty years, pensions would be 34 percent larger than if earnings grew at a steady 5 percent annual rate. And they would be 75 percent larger than pensions available if earnings grew at 2 percent for the first twenty years and 8.1 percent for the second twenty years. These estimates assume that contributions to the defined-contribution pension earned a steady 7 percent return per year.

2. Figure 3–1 shows the replacement rates—the ratio of benefits to the worker's average earnings between the ages of 54 and 58—for successive cohorts of hypothetical "average" male workers. The workers enter the labor force at age 22 and work for forty years. They experience the age-earnings profile of employed men in 1995. Economy-wide real earnings are assumed to grow 2 percent a year. Six percent of earnings are contributed to a defined-contribution pension plan that invests in a mixture of common stocks that yields the average dividend and capital gain of all listed securities in that year. The plan, which imposes no fees or charges, reinvests all dividends, which are free of individual tax when paid. At age 62, workers convert their accumulated savings into annuities based on the expected mortality experience of American men in 1995 and the interest rate on six-month commercial paper in the year when the annuity is purchased. All insurance company fees are ignored.

3. Take, for example, two workers with the same $58,997 average earnings over a forty-year period. One worker's annual earnings start at $30,000 and grow steadily by 3 percent a year. The other's start at $15,000 and grow at 5.8 percent a year. If each is required to contribute 5 percent of earnings to a defined-contribution plan that earns a steady 7 percent return per year, the pension of the first worker will be 28 percent larger than that of the second worker.

4. Government laws and regulations require insurance companies to charge some customers more for annuities and others less than available information on life expectancy warrants. Antidiscrimination laws prohibit race-based differences in annuity prices, even though whites are expected to live longer than blacks. At age 65, life expectancy of white males exceeds that of black males by two years. Accordingly, annuities for white men cost insurance companies more than do annuities sold to blacks. But law requires that the prices must be the same. The result is that blacks must systematically

pay more and whites less than they would if annuity prices were based on average life expectancies. For some classes of insurance, prohibition of race-based price differences works in the opposite way. Blacks are almost twice as likely to become disabled as whites are. Disability insurance premiums based on race-specific disability rates would be higher for blacks than for whites, but such pricing is also prohibited. Gender may be used in setting prices for individual annuities. But it may not be used in determining pension amounts under group annuities.

5. Jeff Brown, "How Should We Insure Longevity Risk in Pensions and Social Security?" Issue Brief, no. 4, Center for Retirement Research at Boston College, August 2000. "In the U.S., inflation-indexed annuities are largely not available to consumers." Brown then goes on to report that TIAA-CREF offers an annuity with substantial, but not complete, inflation protection and that Irish Life of North America offers a true CPI-indexed annuity but no one has bought it.

6. Lawrence Thompson, *Older and Wiser: The Economics of Public Pensions* (Washington, D.C.: Urban Institute Press, 1998), pp. 155–59. The implicit inflation forecast over ten years is the difference between the annual yield to maturity on a ten-year bond and an estimate of the real rate of return. For example, ten-year Treasury index bonds that are fully protected against fluctuations in the consumer price index yielded approximately 3.6 percent in addition to the rate of inflation at the beginning of 2001. On January 4, 2001, for example, the interest rate on inflation-indexed Treasury bonds maturing in 2028 was 3.64 percent, while the interest rate on bonds without inflation protection was 5.5 percent, implying that investors expect inflation to run just under 2 percent a year over the succeeding three decades. Thompson reports: "From the mid 1960s though the mid 1970s, many of the retirees relying on these market predictions would have ended up losing some 20 to 30 percent of their accumulated wealth to inflation not anticipated by the market. Losses would have been the smallest in Germany (averaging 14 percent from 1966 though 1973) and the largest in the United Kingdom (averaging about 76 percent from 1966 through 1973)."

7. Benefits are available to dependent children under the age of 18 and disabled dependent children age 18 or older.

8. Five members of the 1994–96 Advisory Council on Social Security proposed such a dual system. People who worked fewer than thirty-five years would receive a pro-rated portion of the flat benefit.

9. Social Security's income is composed of payroll tax receipts, a portion of the receipts derived from subjecting benefits above certain thresholds to the income tax, general fund transfers, and interest income on trust fund balances.

10. Returns for individual workers vary around this average for several reasons. The most important is that Social Security pays larger benefits

relative to earnings to low earners and members of large families than to high earners and members of small families. If some people get more than average, someone must get less. In addition, projections are sometimes inaccurate. The changes in tax rates or pension rules necessary to reestablish financial balance alter returns of affected workers or pensioners. Congress sometimes adds new benefits—disability insurance in 1956, for example. When such changes occur, new beneficiaries enjoy temporarily inflated returns. They enjoy the same windfall received by people who became eligible for benefits soon after Social Security was enacted. In both cases, people become eligible for expanded benefits after only a brief period of paying the taxes to support those benefits.

11. As enacted in 1935, the Economic Security Act called for the imposition of payroll taxes starting in 1937 and the payment of retirement benefits starting in 1942. In 1939, Congress advanced to 1940 the date when benefits would first be paid. The 1935 law called for accumulation of reserves that would have reached approximately twelve times annual benefit payments by 1970, a sizable reserve although well short of what would have been accumulated under a defined-contribution plan. The 1939 amendments moved Social Security to pay-as-you-go financing. That policy remained in effect until 1977, when legislation called for reserve accumulation to begin. The slowdown in trend economic growth that started in the mid-1970s spoiled those plans. Congressional action in 1983 initiated an era of reserve accumulation.

12. The adjustments could take place by rasing general revenues or curtailing spending elsewhere in the budget and transferring the resultant surplus to the retirement program.

13. Transfers to Social Security also could be financed by increased borrowing. But increased borrowing necessitates either higher taxes or lower spending in the future to pay debt service.

14. "Trust Funds and Federal Funds," *Budget of the United States Government, Fiscal Year 2000, Analytical Perspectives,* 1999, p. 337. A similar view is expressed in Congressional Budget Office, *An Analysis of the President's Budgetary Proposals for the Fiscal Year 2001,* April 2000, p. 61.

15. To the extent that Social Security encourages people to retire earlier than they would if Social Security did not exist, it stimulates saving. If people wish to maintain the same living standard after retirement that they enjoyed while working, increasing the duration of retirement raises the proportion of total lifetime income that will be consumed after earnings have stopped. To finance that consumption the portion of lifetime income consumed while working must be reduced—that is, saving has to increase. Many scholarly studies have addressed the question of whether, on balance, Social Security increases or decreases saving. The evidence is mixed.

16. Steve Stecklow and Sara Callian, "Financial Flop: Social Security Switch in U.K. Is Disastrous: A Caution to the U.S.?" *Wall Street Journal*, August 10, 1998, p. A1.

4

1. For the most part, the two groups are distinct. Most retired, disabled, and survivor beneficiaries do not work, but some engage in part-time work, and a few work full time. Only 3.5 percent of beneficiaries had their pensions reduced or eliminated altogether because of earnings in 1999, the last year before repeal of the earnings test for beneficiaries age 65 or older.

2. Over the 1990s, real per capita GDP grew at an average rate of 2 percent per year. Because the growth of the labor force is expected to slow more than population growth, the Congressional Budget Office, the Social Security actuaries, and the Office of Management and Budget expect per capita growth to average 1.1 to 1.2 percent between 1998 and 2040.

3. David M. Cutler and Ellen Meara, "The Medical Costs of the Young and Old: A Forty-Year Perspective," NBER Working Paper no. 6114, National Bureau of Economic Research, Cambridge, Mass., July 1997.

4. Jonathan Gruber and David Wise, "Social Security Programs and Retirement around the World," NBER Working Paper no. 6134, National Bureau of Economic Research, Cambridge, Mass., August 1997.

5. See Joseph F. Quinn, "Has the Early Retirement Trend Reversed?" paper presented to Retirement Research Consortia, May 20–21, 1999, for an exposition of the view that retirement ages will continue to increase, and Dora L. Costa, *The Evolution of Retirement: An American Economic History, 1880–1990* (Chicago: University of Chicago Press, 1998), for the view that the long-term trends are durable.

6. The age at which unreduced benefits will be paid rises two months a year starting for workers who turn age 62 in 2000 until it reaches 66 for those turning 62 in 2005. For the succeeding twelve years, the age of normal retirement will remain at 66. Then it will be increased two months a year between 2017 and 2022. The increase in the "normal" age for claiming widows' and widowers' benefits begins in 2002 and ends in 2024.

7. There is no earnings test for those age 70 and older. Beneficiaries may receive unlimited amounts from private pensions, rents, royalties, and income from capital.

8. The cost of repealing the retirement test for those over the full-benefits age was neglibible because only a bit more than half of those working and not receiving Social Security at this age will have earnings that exceed $30,000, the level the earnings test will reach in 2002. Furthermore, after

2005, when the delayed retirement credit fully compensates workers for benefits lost because of earnings above the threshold, the earnings test will have been effectively repealed. Repealing the earnings test means that workers receive the same expected lifetime benefits no matter when they retire. An actuarially fair delayed retirement credit has the same effect. However, the psychological effects of repealing the earnings test might well differ from those of an actuarially fair delayed retirement credit.

9. We explain why income testing is inadvisable in Box 7–1.

5

1. This estimate assumes wages grow at 4.3 percent annually and that inflation is 3.3 percent annually, as assumed in the long-range projections for Social Security. The investment return averages 8.8 percent, a rate assumed by some advocates of privatizing Social Security.

2. National Academy of Social Insurance, *Evaluating Issues in Privatization of Social Security: Report of the Panel on Privatization of Social Security*, Washington, D.C., 1998

3. Stephen C. Goss, "Measuring Solvency in the Social Security System," paper presented at the Wharton School, University of Pennsylvania, May 12, 1997.

4. Social Security reserves were approximately $1.1 trillion at the end of 2000—enough to support benefits for only about two and one-half years. Reserve accumulation is projected to continue until 2024. Relative to benefits, reserves will peak in 2015, when they will be equal to about four and one-half years of benefits.

5. For example, some proposals would permit individuals to "opt out" of Social Security, that is, to shift their funds to personal retirement accounts. For reasons set forth in Box 3–6, such an approach is inherently unstable. The problem is that high earners would find it financially more attractive to leave Social Security than would low earners. While payroll taxes are proportional to earnings, Social Security benefits rise less than proportionately with earnings. In addition, high earners are more likely to be familiar with the operation of financial markets and would face proportionately lower administrative charges because their private account balances would be larger. As a result, voluntary withdrawal would leave Social Security with proportionately more low earners and fewer high earners. Since low earners receive larger benefits in relation to their payroll tax payments than do high earners, voluntary withdrawal would create deficits, necessitating one of two responses. The payroll tax rate necessary to support benefits for workers who remain inside the system would have to rise, causing still more

workers to withdraw. Or subsidies from general tax revenues would have to be provided to support the social assistance provided by the Social Security system. What this all means is that the proposal to permit workers to "opt" out of Social Security is not a complete plan. It buries the transition costs that most privatization plans honestly face by failing to analyze the inevitable consequences of permitting workers voluntarily to leave the system.

6. This represents the returns to the average wage worker, not the real return earned on the balances of the trust funds, which is estimated to be 3 percent over the long run.

7. If funds accumulate over a working life of forty years, the average dollar is on deposit for approximately twenty years. A fee of 1 percent of funds on deposits, subtracted twenty times, reduces the balance by approximately 20 percent.

8. If IRAs, Keogh plans, and the cash value of life insurance are excluded, fewer than one in eight families have liquid assets that exceed their annual income. Federal Reserve Board, *Survey of Consumer Finances*, Washington, D.C., 1995.

9. Caroline Daniel, "A Look at . . . The Future of Social Security: Taxing Reforms for British Retirees," *Washington Post*, Outlook, August 9, 1998, p. C3. Mamta Murthi, J. Michael Orszag, and Peter R. Orszag, "Administrative Costs and Individual Accounts from the U.K. Experience," Center on Budget and Policy Priorities, Washington, D.C., March 16, 1999 (http://www.cbpp.org/3-16-99socsec-pr.htm).

10. We assume that, subject to private (or public) offsets, described in the text below, the accumulation of funds in pension funds leads to smaller increases in consumption than do additions to income in other forms.

11. Almost all of the reserves are invested in special Treasury securities not sold to the public. These special issues have an important advantage over publicly held Treasury securities. The Social Security trustees can sell their special issues to the Treasury at par regardless of the current market price of Treasury bonds of the same yield and maturity. This feature spares Social Security a risk that private investors face, of suffering a capital loss if compelled to sell bonds when interest rates were higher and bond prices lower than at issue.

12. B. Douglas Bernheim and Daniel M. Garrett, "The Determinants and Consequences of Financial Education in the Workplace: Evidence from a Survey of Households," NBER Working Paper 5667, Cambridge, Mass., July 1996; Patrick J. Bayer, B. Douglas Bernheim, and John Karl Scholz, "The Effects of Financial Education in the Workplace: Evidence from a Survey of Employers," NBER Working Paper 5655, Cambridge, Mass., July 1996.

13. William G. Gale and John Sabelhaus, "Perspectives on the Household Saving Rate," *Brookings Papers on Economic Activity 1: 1999* (1999), table 4, p. 199.

14. Peter D. Hart Research Associates, "Americans View the Social Security Debate," Washington, D.C., July 1998.

15. These estimates are drawn from Lawrence Thompson, *Older and Wiser: The Economics of Public Pensions* (Washington, D.C., : The Urban Institute Press, 1998), p. 149. Thompson's calculations show that the variability in contribution rates based on the experiences in Germany, Japan, and the United Kingdom would have been somewhat less extreme than those in the United States. Whether contribution rates would have to rise or fall depends on whether growth of wages is accelerating or decelerating and whether interest rates are rising or falling.

16. The costs of disability insurance, which are larger than those of retirement and survivor insurance, are not included in this figure because privatization plans typically do not encompass disability insurance.

17. Before 1995, the Social Security Administration provided reports only to those participants who requested information. As a result of legislation enacted in 1989 and 1990, SSA began sending information on past earnings and estimated benefits to all participants age 60 and older. By 2000, SSA will be required to provide information periodically to all workers age 25 and over who are not receiving benefits.

18. Olivia S. Mitchell, James M. Poterba, and Mark J. Warshawsky, "New Evidence on the Money's Worth of Individual Annuities," NBER Working Paper 6002, National Bureau of Economic Research, Cambridge, Mass., April 1997.

19. Such information would be needed if private account balances were divided upon divorce. If private accounts are treated as the sole property of the worker, divorced women could experience a substantial reduction in retirement incomes compared to the current situation. For more detailed examination of these issues, see National Academy of Social Insurance, *Evaluating Issues in Privatization of Social Security.*

20. One way to counteract this effect would be to impose a tax on funds not used to buy annuities, the proceeds from which would be used to subsidize annuities. The tax would offset the unfavorable selection into the annuity pool.

6

1. The figure is for 1998. In 1996, 12.3 percent of the elderly were poor after including Social Security income but before including other transfer payments. Other cash and in-kind government programs reduce the after-tax poverty rate for the elderly to 9.2 percent. These effects are measured net of Social Security payroll taxes, which reduce incomes and push some below the

poverty threshold. Kathy Porter et al., "Strengths of the Safety Net," Center on Budget and Policy Priorities, Washington, D.C., March 8, 1998, pp. 8, 30, Table A–2.

2. Jonathan Gruber and David Wise, "Social Security Programs and Retirement around the World," NBER Working Paper no. 6134, National Bureau of Economic Research, Cambridge, Mass., August 1997, Table 1. The nations surveyed are Belgium, France, Italy, the Netherlands, the United Kingdom, Germany, Spain, Canada, the United States, Sweden, and Japan. We are not suggesting that the United States should emulate replacement rates or entitlement ages of other countries, which face burdensome growth of costs and will probably be forced to cut benefits. We are observing only that *relative* U.S. benefits are modest.

3. A 1999 retiree who worked full time at the minimum wage received an annual pension of $6,990 if single and $10,485 with a spouse's benefit. In 1999, the poverty threshold was $7,990 for a single person age 65 or older and $10,070 for a couple.

4. Because adjusting millions of pension benefits is a complicated task, the percentage increase in benefits provided in December of each year actually reflects inflation that occurred between the third quarter of the preceding year and the third quarter of the current year.

5. "In the United States, inflation-indexed annuities are largely not available to consumers. Historically, this scarcity was due to the lack of inflation-indexed investments with which life insurance companies could underwrite policies. In 1997, however, the U.S. government introduced Treasury Inflation Protected Securities (TIPS). Since the introduction of these securities, two companies have made inflation-indexed annuities available to consumers. TIAA-CREF, the principal and long-standing retirement system for the nation's education and research sectors, offers a variable annuity linked to an 'Inflation Linked Bond Account.' While this product does not guarantee a fixed real income stream due to several design features, it does offer a very high degree of inflation protection. However, this product is not available outside of the education and research sector. A second company, Irish Life of North America, offers a true CPI-indexed annuity, but as of this writing [August 2000] they had no sales of this product." Jeffrey R. Brown, "How Should We Insure Longevity Risk in Pensions and Social Security?" Issue Brief no. 4, Center for Retirement Research at Boston College, August 2000, p. 12.

6. To be sure, work generates eligibility for disability coverage. An additional benefit is the "disability freeze," which shortens the worker's earnings averaging period for retirement benefits to the number of years already worked. These benefits are valuable, but they account for only a small share of the payroll tax.

7. The lower figure about equals the difference between the poverty threshold for an elderly couple and that for a single older person.

8. Some versions of earnings sharing credit each spouse with more than half of the combined total.

9. After ten years of marriage, divorced spouses are entitled to a spouse or survivor benefit, however far in the past the marriage may have ended. This provision means that a divorced person's pension can depend on the earnings record of a person the beneficiary has not lived with for two or even three decades.

10. If both members of the couple received equal benefits based on their own earnings, the survivor receives a benefit only half of what the couple received. If the couple received a worker's benefit and a spouse's benefit, the survivor receives only the worker's benefit, a drop of one-third. All other cases fall between these two extremes.

11. Federal legislation enacted in 1984 requires that some fraction of the basic pension continue to be paid to the pensioner's widow or widower, unless he or she waives this right in writing.

12. Conversely, age-67 retirees will not receive the increased benefits paid under the old law to people who work past age 65 and have sufficient earnings to be subject to the retirement test.

13. Even if the benefit reduction rate for early retirement is actuarially sound, increasing the age of initial eligibility will reduce costs because those who died between the old and new age thresholds would receive no benefits.

14. If, in 2011, life expectancy at age 20 were 82.7 years, the number of years the average person lived beyond the age at which unreduced benefits were paid would be 15.7 (82.7 minus 67), and the retirement period would constitute one-quarter of adult life (15.7 divided by 62.7 [82.7 minus 20]). If average adult life expectancy were to increase by one year to 83.7, the age at which unreduced benefits were paid would rise to 67 years, nine months.

15. Some have proposed extending the averaging period to 40 years, a change that would eliminate more than 20 percent of the projected long-term deficit. One variant of this proposal would count all lifetime earnings and divide the total by 40. This would boost benefits for those who worked steadily from when they were teenagers to when they retired. Any increase in the averaging period would reduce benefits disproportionately for women and others who do not work continuously.

16. The Consumer Price Index is used to adjust benefits after they are initially calculated. But a wage index based on the growth of earnings covered by the payroll tax is used for two other adjustments. Earnings received in years before a worker turns age 60 are increased by the ratio of average wages in the year the worker turns 60 to average wages in the year the wages were received. The "bend points" in the formula used in computing benefits also are adjusted by the wage index. Benefits are equal to 90 percent of average earnings up to the first "bend point," 32 percent of earnings between the first and second bend point, and 15 percent of earnings above the second bend point.

17. The Congressional Budget Office has estimated that the changes adopted between 1995 and 2002 should reduce the growth rate of the CPI by about 0.7 percentage points a year. Congressional Budget Office, *The Economic and Budget Outlook, Fiscal Years 1999–2008* (Washington, D.C.: U.S. Government Printing Office, 1998), Box 1–2, pp. 8–9. See also Council of Economic Advisers, *The Economic Report of the President, 1998* (Washington, D.C.: U.S. Government Printing Office, 1998), pp. 79–80. For a thorough and accessible review of the issues, the best single source is the six articles in "Symposium: Measuring the CPI," *Journal of Economic Perspectives* 12, no. 1 (Winter 1998): 3–78.

18. The Omnibus Budget Reconciliation Act of 1990 required all state and local workers who were not covered by a pension plan to be in Social Security starting in July 1991.

19. Affected states and localities would have to modify their current pension plans, a manageable task that the federal government performed when its civilian employees hired after December 31, 1983, were brought into Social Security.

20. In fact, general revenues have been used in Social Security in limited ways. The allocation of revenues from income taxation of Social Security benefits is an application of general revenues. So too were payments made to provide Social Security earnings credits for the military. In addition, when minimum Social Security benefits were eliminated in 1981, they were preserved for those born before 1920 and financed through a general revenue transfer.

21. The reduction in the projected deficit depends on the other reforms because they generate larger reserves to invest.

22. This would take the form of a rule change that would establish a point of order requiring a sixty-vote majority to waive.

7

1. James Dao and Alison Mitchell, "Gore Denounces Bush Social Security Plan as Too Risky," *New York Times*, May 17, 2000, p. A-20.

2. The previous edition of this book outlined several additional proposals.

3. If investments yielded exactly the historical average rate of return in every year, no one would receive anything from his or her individual account. The text statement is based on personal communication from Social Security chief actuary, Stephen Goss.

4. Phil Gramm, "Investment-Based Social Security," *Tax Notes,* November 13, 2000, pp. 923–54.

5. This plan was initially crafted by the National Commission on Retirement Policy, a group including members of Congress, leaders from the private sector, and policy analysts. A similar plan was introduced into the House of Representatives by Charles Stenholm (Democrat of Texas) and Jim Kolbe (Republican of Arizona).

6. We use the term "proposal" rather than plan for the ideas set forth by the two presidential candidates during the 2000 presidential campaign. Neither candidate provided a full plan, but both indicated the general directions in which they wished to move.

7. Henry J. Aaron, Alan S. Blinder, Alicia H. Munnell, and Peter R. Orszag, "Governor Bush's Individual Account Proposal: Implications for Retirement Benefits," Issue Brief no. 11, The Century Foundation, New York, 2000 (www.tcf.org or www.socsec.org). The estimated cuts in Social Security benefits embody several assumptions that minimize the size of those cuts. Survivor's benefits are assumed to be cut for workers who move to individual accounts. Administrative cost assumptions are well below those experienced under foreign account systems, although voluntary plans are more costly than foreign mandatory plans to administer.

8. Alternatively, general revenue transfers could be used to reduce the payroll taxes diverted into private accounts, thereby avoiding part or all of the increase in the long-term deficit created by the plan.

9. Dao and Mitchell, "Gore Denounces Bush Social Security Plan as Too Risky."

10. " Long-Range OASDI Financial Effects of the President's Proposal for Strengthening Social Security–Information," memo from Stephen C. Goss to Chief Actuary Harry C. Ballantyne, June 26, 2000.

11. Except for one provision, the Gore proposal for general revenue transfers was identical to one presented by President Clinton on June 20, 2000. The Gore proposal failed to include a Clinton scheme for investing up to 15 percent of the Social Security trust fund in common stocks. Such investments would have further reduced the projected long-term deficit to 0.48 percent of payroll, a combined reduction of 75 percent.

8

1. Congressional Budget Office, *The Long-Term Budget Outlook*, Washington, D.C., 2000.

INDEX

About the Authors

Henry J. Aaron is a senior fellow at the Brookings Institution, where he directed the economic studies program from 1990 through 1996. He is also a member of the Institute of Medicine and the American Academy of Arts and Sciences. He has been a student of Social Security for thirty-five years and chaired the 1979 Advisory Council on Social Security. He is chair of the board of the National Academy of Social Insurance and was president of the Association of Public Policy Management.

Robert D. Reischauer is president of the Urban Institute. He served as director of the Congressional Budget Office from 1989 to 1995. Currently, he is chairman of the Restructuring Medicare for the Long Term project of the National Academy of Social Insurance and a member of the Medicare Payment Advisory Commission. He has testified and written extensively on social insurance policy issues.